HOW TO DOMINATE IN A
WICKED NATION

ALSO FROM REVIVAL TODAY

Dominion Over Sickness and Disease

Boldly I Come: Praying According to God's Word

Twenty Secrets for an Unbreakable Marriage

How to Dominate in a Wicked Nation

Books are available in EBOOK and PAPERBACK through your favorite online book retailer or by request from your local book store.

HOW TO DOMINATE IN A WICKED NATION

LESSONS LEARNED FROM THE LIFE OF ABRAHAM

JONATHAN SHUTTLESWORTH

Book design by eBook Prep: www.ebookprep.com

January 2022
eBook ISBN: 978-1-64457-261-0
Paperback ISBN: 978-1-64457-262-7

Rise UP Publications
644 Shrewsbury Commons Ave, Ste 249
Shrewsbury PA 17361
United States of America
www.riseUPpublications.com
Phone: 866-846-5123

CONTENTS

Nobody who follows the Word of God stays low.

— JONATHAN SHUTTLESWORTH

INTRODUCTION

When Donald Trump lost the 2020 election, you would have thought Jesus died. Christians were posting everywhere on social media that they were depressed, couldn't believe it happened and didn't know what they were going to do.

Elections are important. Who you vote for matters, but the Bible says our spiritual root is in Abraham.

> "Hearken to me, ye that follow after righteousness,
>> ye that seek the Lord: look unto the rock whence
>> ye are hewn, and to the hole of the pit whence ye
>> are digged.
> Look unto Abraham your father, and unto Sarah that
>> bare you: for I called him alone, and blessed him,
>> and increased him.
> For the Lord shall comfort Zion: he will comfort all
>> her waste places; and he will make her
>> wilderness like Eden, and her desert like the

garden of the Lord; joy and gladness shall be found therein, thanksgiving, and the voice of melody."

— ISAIAH 51:1-3 (KJV)

The New Living Translation phrases verse 2 this way: "*Abraham was only one man when I called him. But when I blessed him, he became a great nation.*"

NOT ONE OF MANY

Abraham was not one of 60 million believers in his nation like you are, if you live in the United States. Abraham was the *only* righteous man on the face of the earth, that we know of. He certainly didn't have any righteous friends. He only had one person who tagged along and who wasn't his enemy...his nephew, Lot. Lot chose to settle in Sodom and Gomorrah (Genesis 19) and wasn't really a righteous man.

Abraham settled in Philistia, one of five city-states ruled by the Five Lords, on the abandoned southern coast of Canaan. There, he was as a lone righteous man in a wicked nation. However, Abraham dominated in that wicked nation.

Abraham didn't spend time sharing posts on Instagram about what the Philistines were plotting, or how they offered their children as human sacrifices to false gods. He didn't complain about the opposition he faced.

Abraham focused on what *he* was doing: obeying God. The Bible says, in doing so, Abraham *became* a nation.

"Abraham was only one man when I called him. But
when I blessed him, he became a great nation."

— ISAIAH 51:2

He was *one* man, when God called him. When God finished, Abraham was a *nation* in one man. *God made Abraham a nation contained in one man.* That is your heritage, and that is my heritage!

When I started in the ministry, it was just me—one man. Later, the Lord added Adalis to me. After that, the Lord added Adalis' twin sister, Magalis. Then Patrick. Now we have 17 full-time employees, and that's just the start!

How do I know? Because the DNA of one man becoming a nation lives in those who are the seed of Abraham. (Galatians 3:6-7)

ABRAHAM AND HIS PRIVATE ARMY

Biblical characters are not like what most people imagine them to be. Abraham had a private security force of 318 trained men—men trained to fight; men who Abraham led into battle. (Genesis 14) Abraham was trained to fight as well. He was a stone-cold killer that expected the same of his men.

There were no police to call where Abraham lived. There was no 9-1-1 service in Philistia. Abraham had to protect what God gave him, and he did so with a trained army so powerful that when Kings went to war, they asked Abraham to come and help.

A nation contained in one man, just as Jesus spoke of the mustard seed.

"It is like a mustard seed planted in the ground. It is

the smallest of all seeds, but it becomes the
largest of all garden plants; it grows long
branches, and birds can make nests in its shade."

— MARK 4: 31-32

ANSWERING THE CALL

When Abraham was in his seventies, he was still living in his father's household. The moment he answered the Lord and chose to believe in the promise, the blessing began providing for many people.

The Lord had said to Abram, "Go from your country,
    your people and your father's household to the
    land I will show you.
I will make you into a great nation, and I will bless
    you; I will make your name great, and you will
    be a blessing.
I will bless those who bless you, and whoever curses
    you I will curse; and all peoples on earth will be
    blessed through you."
So Abram went, as the Lord had told him;

— GENESIS 12: 1-4

Abraham didn't become a nation hundreds of years later. He was a nation in one man, in his *own* lifetime. The many families traveling with him drew their income and livelihoods from what Abraham produced.

"Listen to me, all who hope for deliverance—all who
seek the Lord! Consider the rock from which you
were cut, the quarry from which you were mined."

— ISAIAH 51:1

The key to walking in victory, to becoming a nation in one man, is
to *"consider the rock from which you were cut."*

THIS IS YOUR HERITAGE

The secret to staying in victory is to consider yourself the spiritual
seed of Abraham. Which—given that's what God says to do—
makes sense that the Devil wants you to concentrate on the
opposite…you're Black, Hispanic, White, Asian, etcetera.

To the spiritual man who follows the Word, ethnicity never enters
the equation. Ethnic background means nothing. Spiritual lineage is
everything.

For you know that God paid a ransom to save you
from the empty life you inherited from your
ancestors. And it was not paid with mere gold or
silver, which lose their value. It was the precious
blood of Christ, the sinless, spotless Lamb
of God.

— 1 PETER 1:18-19

Whatever you inherited from your ethnicity is an empty life.
Christ's blood is required to deliver you from what came from that

lineage. Today, everybody wants to know where they came from—their lineage.

"Oh, I found out I'm Irish."

What are you going to do? Take a trip with your wife to Ireland and eat boiled potatoes and drink at a pub, so you can really *feel* connected to your roots?

That's the total opposite of what God said to do.

God said you are to disconnect from your ethnic background and plug into the fact that you are the seed of Abraham. That doesn't mean throw on a prayer shawl and take a trip to Israel so you can touch the wailing wall—which Abraham never touched. God wants you to connect with the *spiritual* DNA of Abraham.

> Even as Abraham believed God, and it was
> accounted to him for righteousness.
> Know ye therefore that they which are of faith, the
> same are the children of Abraham.
>
> — GALATIANS 3:6-7 (KJV)

Abraham's righteousness and blessing were not obtained by the garments he wore or the land he lived on, or the places he went. Abraham's blessing was attained by faith—faith in God, and faith in His Word. That is how every overcomer lives, by the faith of Abraham.

I don't see myself as Jonathan Shuttlesworth, 33% Polish-American. I see myself as the seed of Abraham, and everything God promised to Abraham belongs to me.

Why? Because those who are in faith are the same as the children of Abraham.

When that revelation comes alive in you, you'll start distancing yourself from the struggles and begin turning into a nation.

I want you to know this right now: The potential to become a one-man or a one-woman nation is in you!

When that potential grows into an idea that you put into action, you will soon need someone to help handle the money, then a second person to take care of another aspect of the business, and before long an army of people will be attached to you because that's the fruit of the Abrahamic DNA—the DNA that lives in every believer.

If you want to walk in victory and deliverance, consider where you came from.

Say it: *"I come from the rock of Abraham. I was mined from that quarry. That's who I am. I'm not an abuse victim. I'm not somebody who battles depression. I am the seed of Abraham. I'm a Prince of God on this earth, and everything that God promised Abraham belongs to me."*

As you begin to take the shape of a nation, simply by the nature of your spiritual DNA, you will dominate. A dog doesn't have to try to bark, a rooster doesn't have to try to crow, a cow doesn't have to try to moo. And somebody who operates in their spiritual DNA, doesn't have to try to become a dominating force on Earth. It's in their DNA. It happens on its own.

Say this out loud: *"It's in my DNA to dominate."*

ABRAHAM OWNED HIS OWN ECONOMY

As a nation, Abraham also had his own economy. He had his own gold. He had his own silver. He had his own livestock. He had his own water source. He was a nation contained in one man. When God was finished with him, he was a mighty nation. Not just a nation, but a *mighty* nation, with his own military, his own people-group, and his own economy.

There are men, today, who are a nation in one man. Most are not even operating under the blessing of God. They're just fully utilizing the capacity God put in human beings.

Who would you rather be? The President of The Central African Republic or Mark Zuckerberg? From a wealth standpoint, Mark Zuckerberg blows away the nation of The Central African Republic.

CLAIM WHAT'S YOURS

God put the capacity to become a nation inside of *you*, but it is the blessing of God that brings that alive. When you understand that, you don't care what a particular political party is planning.

Do you think no wicked plans were being made where Abraham lived? It was an *extremely* wicked land. There was no Gospel in it. No blood of Jesus that had been shed.

The dominating force God placed inside Abraham overwhelmed the opposing forces that stood against him. What God has placed in you can overwhelm the opposing forces surrounding you! I want to remind you that the blessing from God was not just for Abraham; that same blessing extends to you and me.

> In the same way, "Abraham believed God, and God
> counted him as righteous because of his faith."
> The real children of Abraham, then, are those who
> put their faith in God.
>
> — GALATIANS 3:6-7

Write that down. Not just the reference, but the whole text. Put it where you will see it, read it, and say it every day. *The real children of Abraham are those who put their faith in God. The true seed of Abraham are those who put their faith in God.*

You don't have to be a certain percentage "Jewish," or dress up like you're from mid-20th century Israel, or walk around in tanned, sun-bleached robes, carrying a worn wooden staff in one hand, while leather knotted sandals rub your feet raw, in order to activate God's blessing!

Activating God's Blessing is not about where you came from, or about the clothing you wear, the language you speak, the suffering you endure, the color of your skin, or the nation where you live. It's about your faith in God!

The New King James Version puts Galatians 3:7-9 this way...

> Therefore know that only those who are of faith are
> sons of Abraham. And the Scripture, foreseeing
> that God would justify the Gentiles by faith,
> preached the gospel to Abraham
> beforehand, saying, "In you all the nations shall
> be blessed." So then those who are of faith are
> blessed with believing Abraham.
>
> — GALATIANS 3:7-9 (NKJV)

17

Galatians 3 makes it abundantly clear. You are not receiving a knock-off version of God's Blessing. You get the whole thing because of your faith.

Galatians Chapter 3 starting at verse 8 in the NIV version says...

> Scripture foresaw that God would justify the Gentiles by faith, and announced the gospel in advance to Abraham: "All nations will be blessed through you." So those who rely on faith are blessed along with Abraham, the man of faith.
> For all who rely on the works of the law are under a curse, as it is written: "Cursed is everyone who does not continue to do everything written in the Book of the Law." Clearly no one who relies on the law is justified before God, because "the righteous will live by faith." The law is not based on faith; on the contrary, it says, "The person who does these things will live by them." Christ redeemed us from the curse of the law by becoming a curse for us, for it is written: "Cursed is everyone who is hung on a pole." He redeemed us in order that the Blessing given to Abraham might come to the Gentiles through Christ Jesus, so that by faith we might receive the promise of the Spirit.

> — GALATIANS 3: 8-14 NIV

Continuing to verses 26 through 29...

> So in Christ Jesus you are all children of

God through faith, for all of you who were
baptized into Christ have clothed yourselves with
Christ. There is neither Jew nor Gentile, neither
slave nor free, nor is there male and female, for
you are all one in Christ Jesus. If you belong to
Christ, then you are Abraham's seed, and
heirs according to the promise.

— GALATIANS 3: 26-29 NIV

Everything God promised Abraham belongs to you. The blessing
has been extended to you and to me. You can access it, whatever
race you are. You can access it, whatever nation you live in. This
blessing works regardless of nationality, regardless of ethnicity,
whether you are male or female. When you activate God's blessing
through faith, it's impossible to get hung up on gender problems.
It's impossible to get hung up on racial divides. It's impossible to
get hung up on where you live.

That's the reason why I'm writing this book.

It's easy to tell by the way Christians react to problems in their
lives, in their nations, and in the world, that most possess *zero*
understanding that they're the seed of Abraham, AND that
everything God promised Abraham belongs to them.

Say it: *Everything God promised Abraham belongs to me.*

Not, everything Abraham had is going to be given to me.

Everything Abraham had has already been given to me.

Stop getting hung up on what a political candidate or government
official says or does; or doesn't do. Don't let any political party's
plans derail your faith. What they have, or think they have, can

NOT derail what God has given you. What you have, what lives inside of you, can overwhelm everything they're planning to do or may do.

How to Dominate in a Wicked Nation: Lessons Learned From The Life of Abraham.

Let's get started.

LESSON 1

ABRAHAM BELIEVED HE WAS BLESSED

Now the Lord had said unto Abram, Get thee out of
thy country, and from thy kindred, and from thy
father's house, unto a land that I will shew thee:
And I will make of thee a great nation , and I will
bless thee, and make thy name great; and thou
shalt be a blessing: And I will bless them that
bless thee, and curse him that curseth thee: and in
thee shall all families of the earth be blessed.

— GENESIS 12:1-3 (KJV)

I want you to get this concept down...the *whole* concept: *I am a
nation contained in one man.*

If you play your cards right, there should be streets named after you
and at least one massive property that belongs to you when you die.

That didn't just happen with Abraham and Isaac and Jacob. You can visit the late Kenneth Hagen's ministry right now. ...huge property, huge church, huge Bible college; all active and alive.

The Oral Roberts University and Prayer Tower are all huge buildings. He was building a faith city.

John Alexander Dowie founded the town of Zion, Illinois with his own town fathers, buildings, and school system.

There are currently ministries overseas, with their own banks.

A nation contained in one man.

I really feel like much of the pressure—the pushback—that Christians get in this world (for being Christians), is allowed by God, *because* He doesn't want us using heathen platforms.

Maybe God doesn't want YouTube taking 30% of every offering given to our ministry. Maybe God is taking these easy solutions away, or allowing these solutions to be taken away, so that the Church will finally choose to live like their father, Abraham—develop their own banking, develop their own payment processing, develop their own media platforms separate from the world. Why are we always trying to jam ourselves onto platforms and into companies that hate our God, hate us, and hate the Bible? It's time for a new generation of Abrahams to arise!

Back to Genesis 12, in verse 2, *"And I will make of thee a great nation."*

Read that again. *A great nation.* Not *a* nation. A *great* nation. The capacity to become a great nation lives in me and lives in you.

"I will bless thee, and make thy name great; and thou shalt be a blessing: And I will bless them that bless thee, and curse him that

curseth thee." And by curse, God means kill. He'll kill those who curse you.

"And in thee shall all families of the earth be blessed." Did it work? Did God keep His promise to Abraham?

> And Abram was very rich in cattle, in silver, and in gold.
>
> — GENESIS 13:2 (KJV)

Abraham believed he was blessed. How can you know that?

> And he believed in the LORD; and he counted it to him for righteousness.
>
> — GENESIS 15:6 (KJV)

Abraham believed the Word, put his faith in the Word, and the Word tells us that he was blessed. Yet, today, Christians gravitate toward curses. If you announced a conference focused on breaking generational curses in the Church, the event would pack out. On the other hand, if you speak on the blessing for 90 seconds, people get up and leave. "He's one of those blessing preachers."

People gravitate to the curse. They'll deliberate, speculate, create a ten-point outline on a curse's "whys-and-wherefores," all while shunning the Blessing. I don't know why that is. I've never understood most human beings, and I've pretty much quit trying.

But that's not what Abraham did. Abraham heard God tell him, *"I'll bless you and make you a blessing."* And he believed those things that were spoken unto him.

Abraham did not believe he was cursed.

Abraham believed he was blessed.

Do you believe you are blessed?

ABRAHAM EXPECTED A REWARD FOR OBEYING GOD

There are many Christians who expect trouble for serving God, but Abraham expected a reward. Where does your expectation lie? Are you looking for *trouble* every time you serve the Lord? Or do you expect a *reward* for obeying His direction? Here's what many Christians hear from the pulpit. "How many of you know when you serve the Lord, it's not going to be easy?"

"Friends will turn against you." Friends turn against you anyway.

"People will talk about you." People talk about you anyway.

> ...In the world ye shall have tribulation: but be of
> good cheer; I have overcome the world.
>
> — JOHN 16:33 (KJV)

Where was your focus when you read this verse? Did you see only the trouble and tribulation (facts), or did you see the command to "be of good cheer," followed by the reward?

Try again: *"In this world, you will have tribulation* [fact]. *But be of good cheer* [command], *for I have overcome the world* [the reward, making you more than a conqueror]."

Whatever you talk about the most—the fact, the command or the blessing—you give the power to increase and multiply in your life. Where is your focus?

If you follow the average Christian on social media, you'll discover most don't know how to use their words or their minds to amplify the blessing of God contained in His Word. Instead, they focus on the trials, the tribulations, the curses of this world while ignoring— even running from— the blessing God said is already theirs for walking in obedience and faith.

In this world, you *will* have trouble. But be of good cheer, for the blessing overwhelms the trouble.

Read that again. Write it down. Make it your focus. *The blessing overwhelms the trouble.*

Trouble never overwhelmed Abraham's blessing.

Abraham went through much trouble—lots of it. Some of it was his own making. But still, what was against him could not overwhelm his blessing.

> Trouble chases sinners, while blessings reward the
> righteous.
>
> — PROVERBS 13:21.

Make this your memory verse for today.

I don't know about you, but that's not what I was taught growing up in church. They might as well have flipped the verse around: Trouble chases the righteous while blessings reward sinners. "I could be out in the world, making money, having all kinds of nice cars and things. But when you get saved, how many of you know the Devil attacks?"

That's not what the Bible teaches.

The Bible teaches that trouble *does not* chase the righteous. Trouble chases sinners. Blessings chase the righteous. Until you get that straight, you'll be one of those who lift their hand every Sunday to be kept in prayer.

Say it: *Trouble is not allowed to chase me. Blessings are assigned to chase me.*

As far as your day-to-day life is concerned, it does not matter what the Bible says. What matters is what you believe the Bible says, what you meditate on, and what you speak that's in the Bible.

> For as he thinketh in his heart, so is he: Eat and
> drink, saith he to thee; but his heart is not with
> thee.
>
> — PROVERBS 23:7 (KJV)

God wants everybody to be saved (2 Peter 3:9), but billions are on their way to hell right now. Why? Because that part of God's Word —salvation—doesn't work and will not come to fruition until they *believe* the Word and *speak* the Word.

> That if thou shalt confess with thy mouth the Lord
> Jesus, and shalt believe in thine heart that God
> hath raised him from the dead, thou shalt be
> saved.
>
> — ROMANS 10:9 (KJV)

For many people reading this, there was a time in your life when you were far from God. Then somebody shared God's Word with you, you believed it, you confessed it, and it turned your whole life around. That's how Salvation works.

That's how it works with every other part of the Bible, including healing, peace, and financial multiplication. Until you *believe* it, meditate on it, make it your focus, and *speak* it out of your mouth, the Bible doesn't work for you.

The first step to moving in this direction...stop gravitating to the curse.

"Well, I just think I'm under a generational curse."

STOP thinking like that!

The Bible says Abraham's blessing belongs to you. Abraham wasn't cursed.

"I mean, I just have this generational curse. I know I do."

Really? What generational curse is upon Abraham's bloodline?

How can you be under a generational curse when you're the seed of Abraham?

The only way to come under a generational curse is to disobey Isaiah 51 and 2 Peter 1 and consider yourself of the lineage of your earthly family instead of your spiritual father, Abraham.

Was Abraham an alcoholic?

Did Abraham battle suicidal thoughts?

Was Abraham abusive?

Those things don't run in Abraham's family, and you are in that family.

Say this: *"I'm not under the curse. Jesus set me free. For poverty, I have wealth. For sickness, I have health. I'm not under the curse."*

When someone asks, "How many of you need prayer? How many of you have a need? How many of you need a breakthrough?" stop responding on autopilot. You don't need a breakthrough. You carry breakthrough. Write that down. Put it where you will read it every day. *"I don't need a breakthrough. I carry breakthrough."*

ABRAHAM BELIEVED HE WAS BLESSED TO BE A BLESSING

Abraham not only believed he was blessed, he believed he was blessed to be a blessing to others because of what God told him.

> And I will make of thee a great nation, and I will
>   bless thee, and make thy name great; and thou
>   shalt be a blessing: And I will bless them that
>   bless thee, and curse him that curseth thee: and in
>   thee shall all families of the earth be blessed.

> — GENESIS 12:2-3 (KJV)

If you believe this scripture, then it's impossible to see yourself in need. You're not only blessed, but you have an overflow of blessing to meet the needs of people who are hurting.

I'm not a person who is hurting. I'm blessed. God didn't give me just enough blessing for me. Like Abraham, He blessed me and makes me a blessing to others.

If you've followed my ministry for any time, you've never heard me say, "we have a great need. We really need your help." I'm not in need.

I'm blessed. And the blessing is God's answer to needs. Not only my needs, but for others needs as well. I don't need food. I feed people. I don't need money. I provide money for others who are hurting.

Abraham believed not only that he was blessed, but that the blessing was so strong, it made him a blessing to others.

> Therefore it is of faith, that it might be by grace; to
> the end the promise might be sure to all the seed;
> not to that only which is of the law, but to that
> also which is of the faith of Abraham; who is the
> father of us all, (As it is written, I have made thee
> a father of many nations,) before him whom he
> believed, even God, who quickeneth the dead,
> and calleth those things which be not as though
> they were.
>
> — ROMANS 4:16-17 (KJV)

Abraham believed he was blessed.

Abraham believed he was blessed to be a blessing.

Abraham spoke the blessing by calling those things that *were not* as *though they we*re.

When God changed Abram's name to Abraham, He changed his name in that language from "exalted father" to "father of many nations".

Abraham began calling himself "father of many nations" *before* he fathered a single child. He called those things that were not as though they were. Abraham *spoke* the blessing every time he said the new name which God had given him.

You don't wait until you're rich to call yourself rich.

You don't wait until you feel blessed to call yourself blessed.

You don't wait until you're strong to call yourself strong.

Let the weak *say* I am strong. (Joel 3:10, KJV)

Abraham *spoke* the blessing.

Abraham called those things which were not as though they were.

You're never wrong when you quote God.

Say it: *I am blessed.*

> "You will be blessed when you come in and blessed
> when you go out."
>
> — DEUTERONOMY 28:6 (NIV)

Say it: *I am healed.*

> But He was wounded for our transgressions, He was
> bruised for our iniquities; The chastisement for
> our peace was upon Him, And by His stripes we
> are healed.
>
> — ISAIAH 53:5 (NKJV)

Say it: *I am strong.*

> Beat your plowshares into swords and your pruning
> hooks into spears. Let the weakling say, "I am
> strong!"

> — JOEL 3:10 (KJV)

Say it: *I have joy unspeakable, and am full of glory.*

> Though you have not seen him, you love him; and
> even though you do not see him now, you believe
> in him and are filled with an inexpressible and
> glorious joy.

> — 1 PETER 1:8 (NIV)

Say it: *I am wise*

> If any of you lack wisdom, let him ask of God, that
> giveth to all men liberally, and upbraideth not;
> and it shall be given him.

> — JAMES 1:5, (KJV)

Say it: *I have the mind of Christ.*

> But the natural man receiveth not the things of the
> Spirit of God: for they are foolishness unto him:
> neither can he know them, because they are
> spiritually discerned. But he that is spiritual
> judgeth all things, yet he himself is judged of no

man. For who hath known the mind of the Lord,
that he may instruct him? But we have the mind
of Christ.

— 1 CORINTHIANS 2:14-16 (KJV)

Abraham's blessing is an irreversible blessing.

> "Listen, I received a command to bless;
> God has blessed, and I cannot reverse it!
> No misfortune is in his plan for Jacob;
> no trouble is in store for Israel.
> For the LORD their God is with them;
> he has been proclaimed their king.
> God brought them out of Egypt;
> for them he is as strong as a wild ox.
> No curse can touch Jacob;
> no magic has any power against Israel.
> For now it will be said of Jacob,
> 'What wonders God has done for Israel!'"

— NUMBERS 23:20-23

Abraham knew you could not curse what God has blessed.

Every plan, like the one underway between Balaak (a prophet of Go), and Balak (the King of Moab who was attempting to bribe Balaam to curse the Israelites in Numbers 23), had no capacity to succeed. In fact, the more Balak tried to bribe Balaam with silver and gold, the greater God poured out His blessing upon Abraham's seed.

Here's how it ended:

> God brought them out of Egypt; for them he is as
>   strong as a wild ox. He devours all the nations
>   that oppose him, breaking their bones in pieces,
>   shooting them with arrows.
> Like a lion, Israel crouches and lies down; like a
>   lioness, who dares to arouse her?
> Blessed is everyone who blesses you, O Israel, and
>   cursed is everyone who curses you."
> King Balak flew into a rage against Balaam. He
>   angrily clapped his hands and shouted, "I called
>   you to curse my enemies! Instead, you have
>   blessed them three times. Now get out of here!
>   Go back home! I promised to reward you richly,
>   but the LORD has kept you from your reward."
> Balaam told Balak, "Don't you remember what I told
>   your messengers?
> I said, 'Even if Balak were to give me his palace
>   filled with silver and gold, I would be powerless
>   to do anything against the will of the LORD.' I
>   told you that I could say only what the LORD
>   says! Now I am returning to my own people. But
>   first let me tell you what the Israelites will do to
>   your people in the future."
>
> — NUMBERS 24:8-14

If Abraham were alive right now, he would spend no time dwelling on what a particular political party is planning, what a president's planning, or a corporation's planning. They can plan whatever they want. You can't curse who God has blessed.

So, why do some Christians say other Christians can curse them with their words? I don't know. Because they gravitate to the curse and not the blessing?

Anyone can say whatever they want about me, and it'll come back on the person who said it. If every witch in India, Africa, and Canada were standing outside of my office right now cursing me, I'd simply wave at them and wouldn't even spend a moment in prayer about it. Why? Because God said, "I will bless those who bless you. And I will curse anyone who curses you."

He didn't say, *"If you pray about it, I'll do it."* Or, *"If you pray in tongues as hard as you can, I'll do it."* He'll do it for free.

When you believe you possess Abraham's blessing, anyone who curses you will provoke a curse from God upon their own head without your permission. There's literally nothing to worry about.

That's why the Bible says not to worry or be anxious, or have anxiety about anything.

> Don't worry about anything; instead, pray about
> everything. Tell God what you need, and thank
> him for all he has done. Then you will experience
> God's peace, which exceeds anything we can
> understand. His peace will guard your hearts and
> minds as you live in Christ Jesus.
>
> — PHILIPPIANS 4:6-7

LESSON 2

ABRAHAM NEVER BELIEVED "THEY" COULD STOP HIM

According to socio-economic studies, one of the main differences between rich men and poor men is that the poor talk about what "they" are doing to "us". On the other hand, the rich talk about what they personally plan to accomplish.

Having your eyes on what your enemy is doing keeps you poor and defeated. Having a plan from God to go forward keeps you in victory.

Abraham never believed there was a "they" who could stop him.

"Did you hear what *they*'re doing?"

"Did you hear *they*'re going to make vaccines mandatory?"

"Did you hear *they*'re not going to allow us to travel?"

"Did you hear that *they*'re going to turn every Walmart into a concentration camp if you don't get the vaccine?"

Abraham never believed there was a "they" who could stop him.

ABRAHAM NEVER SPENT TIME TALKING "WORRY TALK"

"I don't know what we're going to do."

"I don't know how we're going to make it."

"I just feel like these next four years are going to be very difficult years with this administration."

Do you talk like this?

Do you allow your mind to think like this?

Is this your focus on social media for all to see and read?

You never read about Abraham talking like this.

ABRAHAM DIDN'T SPEND TIME PRAYING "WORRY PRAYERS"

What prayers do you pray?

Personally, I can't work up enough worry inside of me to pray about what politicians are planning to do to the Church. Why? Because whatever plan they have, or think they have, is already destined to fail.

Abraham didn't spend time praying "worry prayers".

Has it ever occurred to you, when hearing someone pray, that what you're getting are layers of unbelief sandwiched between "Dear Heavenly Father" and "in Jesus' name"?

What is the focus of your prayer life? Worry, doubt, and fear? Or the power of Christ in you, the hope of glory?

ABRAHAM SAW HIMSELF AS A RULER

When the world leaders of Abraham's time planned to go to battle, they consulted Abraham (Genesis 14). Abraham saw himself on the same level as world leaders, not under them.

When I hear Christians talk today, many sound and act like serfs from the 13th century; barely surviving under the dominion of some evil King who can do anything he wants to them.

"Did you hear what *they*'re planning? Did you hear what *they*'re doing?"

Stop thinking that way. Stop talking that way. You are the seed of Abraham! Abraham didn't talk about what "they" are doing. Abraham saw himself on their level. Not under them.

The "don't tread on me" mentality was birthed in the United States of America when the colonialists' refused to be under the lordship (kingship) of another human being—this foundation can be seen in Isaiah 54:17.

Here's another important cornerstone to understanding the power within you.

> All praise to God, the Father of our Lord Jesus
>   Christ, who has blessed us with every spiritual
>   blessing in the heavenly realms because we are
>   united with Christ.
>
> — EPHESIANS 1:3

> I also pray that you will understand the incredible
>   greatness of God's power for us who believe
>   him. This is the same mighty power that raised

Christ from the dead and seated him in the place of honor at God's right hand in the heavenly realms Now he is far above any ruler or authority or power or leader or anything else—not only in this world but also in the world to come.

— EPHESIANS 1:19-21

What is Christ far above?

…any ruler.

…any authority.

…any power.

…any leader.

…or anything else.

…not only in this world but also in the world to come.

God has put all things under the authority of Christ and has made him head over all things for the benefit of the church. And the church is his body; it is made full and complete by Christ, who fills all things everywhere with himself. In the mind of God, there is no difference between Christ and the Christian. Christ is the head. We are the body. We've been made one with Christ.

— EPHESIANS 1:22-23

That's strong language, but that's not my problem. God wrote it that way. I'll say it again. In the mind of God, there is *no difference* between Christ and the Christian. He is the head, we are the body. We've been made one with Christ and *seated together* with Him *far above* all rulers, all powers, all authority in this world.

They're not over my head.

They're not eye-to-eye with me.

They're *under* my feet.

If Satan is under my feet (Romans 16:20), how much further under my feet are all the people who work for Satan? Every witch, every sorcerer, every demon-possessed politician who hates the Church and hates Christians…they're under my feet.

Have you ever noticed that when people—Christians especially—talk about politics, the cowards love to quote Romans 13? Let me introduce you to another 13, Acts 13.

> Afterward they traveled from town to town across
>   the entire island until finally they reached
>   Paphos, where they met a Jewish sorcerer, a false
>   prophet named Bar-Jesus. He had attached
>   himself to the governor, Sergius Paulus, who was
>   an intelligent man. The governor invited
>   Barnabas and Saul to visit him, for he wanted to
>   hear the word of God. But Elymas, the sorcerer
>   (as his name means in Greek), interfered and
>   urged the governor to pay no attention to what
>   Barnabas and Saul said. He was trying to keep
>   the governor from believing.
>
>   — ACTS 13:6-8

Now, Bar-Jesus wasn't some snaggle-tooth, rag-wrapped conjuror who smelled of three-day-old urine, feces, and alcohol. He was a sharp-robed, well-sandaled man who operated within a political house and who had successfully attached himself to the governor.

Paul saw through the money and laid out the truth.

> Saul, also known as Paul, was filled with the Holy
> Spirit, and he looked the sorcerer in the eye.
> Then he said, "You son of the devil, full of every
> sort of deceit and fraud, and enemy of all that is
> good! Will you never stop perverting the true
> ways of the Lord? Watch now, for the Lord has
> laid his hand of punishment upon you, and you
> will be struck blind. You will not see the sunlight
> for some time." Instantly mist and darkness came
> over the man's eyes, and he began groping
> around begging for someone to take his hand and
> lead him.
> When the governor saw what had happened, he
> became a believer, for he was astonished at the
> teaching about the Lord.

— ACTS 13:9-12

Paul, who wrote Ephesians Chapter 1, acts out his belief here in Acts 13, pulling no punches and making no apologies. In the natural, the politically connected sorcerer was above Paul in every way. But in the spiritual realm, Paul was far above that sorcerer and proved it in word and deed.

Abraham saw himself on the level of world leaders.

Paul knew all his enemies were under his feet.

What do you believe? I'm not asking what does it look like, feel like, and seem like to you. What do you believe? Where are you choosing to put your faith?

As a man thinketh in his heart, so is he. (Proverbs 23:7)

By the way, two of the other 10 differences between a rich man and a poor man are:

A rich man faces his fears and focuses on a reward.

A poor man focuses on the risk and runs.

LESSON 3

ABRAHAM NEVER LOOKED TO A "THEY" TO HELP HIM

M ost of the body of Christ is either concerned about a group trying to hurt them or looking for a group to help them. Abraham didn't *believe* there was a "they" who could stop him. Abraham didn't *need* a "they" to help him!

You can shout and dance in church every Sunday morning, but if your focus for the next six days is sharing Instagram stories about how the global elitists are taking over America, then you're a worry-minded Christian who happens to attend a church. You can be a winner and a champion all seven days of every week *if* you will change your focus.

Here's the King of Sodom (of Sodom and Gomorrah) attempting to negotiate with Abraham after Abraham returned victorious from battle...

> The king of Sodom said to Abram, "Give back my
> people who were captured. But you may keep for
> yourself all the goods you have recovered."

> Abram replied to the king of Sodom, "I solemnly
> swear to the Lord, God Most High, Creator of
> heaven and earth, that I will not take so much as
> a single thread or sandal thong from what
> belongs to you. Otherwise you might say, 'I am
> the one who made Abram rich.' I will accept only
> what my young warriors have already eaten, and
> I request that you give a fair share of the goods to
> my allies—Aner, Eshcol, and Mamre"
>
> — GENESIS 14:21-24

Abraham knew the source and the power of his blessing.

Reread Abraham's response.

> "...I will not take so much as a single thread or
> sandal thong from what belongs to you.
> Otherwise you might say, 'I am the one who
> made Abram rich.'"

When the Covid19 lockdown hit in 2020, the US Government offered what they called a PPP loan, the Paycheck Protection Program. Businesses that received PPP loans were handed two-and-a-half months of the business's total payroll. Zero-interest. It was *like* free money.

I had one minister, whom I love and who is incredibly wise, say to me, "Jonathan, you're stupid if you don't take that money." With 17 employees on the ministry's payroll at that time, I could have received a lot of money from the US Government. And on paper, there was no reason to not take it. The loan was even being touted as the government's attempt to help churches.

Genesis 14:23 instantly popped up in my spirit. *"I will not take so much as a single thread or sandal thong from what belongs to you. Otherwise you might say, 'I am the one who made Abram rich.'"*

Who did I trust more? The God of my blessing or a political system dangling a few "free" dollars in my face? The answer came quickly. I don't want, I don't need, any money from any government. I just want them to stay out of my way. No one is getting any credit, but My God. You *cannot* walk in Abraham's blessing when you entangle your money with the government. This principle is eternal. This principle will never fade.

Years ago, United States Bible colleges wanted to accept federal and state-funded financial aid so their students could receive government loans to help pay tuition. Then those colleges could increase the amount of tuition charged without losing students because the students could use inexpensive loans and grants to pay for the increase. On the surface, it looked innocuous. But I wrote, "Bible colleges will rue the day they accepted federal money. Anything the government gives you comes at a high price."

Now, those Bible colleges are fighting the government for the right to enforce Biblical guidelines on their own campuses. Instead of following God's principles, those Bible colleges are forced to provide transgender bathrooms and allow homosexual couples as students on their campus.

You *cannot* walk in Abraham's blessing and entangle your money with the government. Like Abraham, focus on God, alone. I've heard many Christians claim that blessing will turn your heart against God. Did God's blessing turn Abraham's heart against God? No. The blessing caused Abraham to *focus* on God alone and refuse any manipulative help from wicked people.

How many Christians today vote for politicians who kill babies so they can keep their welfare check or some other government benefit that's being threatened? They allow themselves to be manipulated by the king of Sodom and, in return, sell out the principles of the Bible for what? A little bit of "free" money that will cost them so much more when election time rolls around again.

The true seed of Abraham knows, trusts, and believes the source of their blessing and tells the government to keep their "free" handouts, lest the king of Sodom say, "I made Abraham rich."

God told Abraham in Genesis 12:1-3, "*Leave your native country, your relatives, and your father's family, and go to the land that I will show you. I will make you into a great nation. I will bless you and make you famous, and you will be a blessing to others. I will bless those who bless you and curse those who treat you with contempt. All the families on earth will be blessed through you.*" Abraham obeyed, and just two chapters later, he knew he was on the top and didn't want anybody to take credit for it.

The government can't hurt me. The government can't help me. My blessing doesn't come from below. My blessing comes from above. And who God has blessed, no government can curse, and who God has blessed requires no help from the government. I don't need the government. But they sure need me. They don't think they do, but when we all get out of here (1 Thessalonians 6:16), seven years later, the entire world economy will fall on itself.

How do I know? You are the light of the world. (Matthew 5:14) You are the salt of the earth. (Matthew 5:13) They don't keep us from rotting. We keep *them* from rotting.

Abraham never looked to a "they" for help. Allow this seed to enter your heart. Make it your focus. Don't allow your mind to drift to carnal thinking, natural thinking. Stop identifying yourself by your fleshly root, by the color of your skin, your nationality, the place where you live, your past, or your gender.

Choose to see yourself as the seed of Abraham, an heir according to the promise. You don't need to drive a Bentley, sport an Armani and a spare, or have a closet full of Jimmy Choos. You certainly don't need to go around blabbing, "Oh, I'm the seed of Abraham." You do, however, need to *see* yourself that way and carry yourself that way. That's why I wear suits when I preach.

Care for the car, the clothing and the possessions you do have. Carry yourself like a Prince. Like a Queen. Like Abraham did. Look like somebody worth knowing. Look like somebody with Jesus on the inside of them, because that's who you are. You are the seed of Abraham.

> "I have made you the father of many nations." This happened because Abraham believed in the God who brings the dead back to life and who creates new things out of nothing.
>
> — ROMANS 4:17

No matter how you feel, own it, live it, be it every day.

LESSON 4

CONSIDER YOUR SPIRITUAL HERITAGE

"Listen to me, all who hope for deliverance all who
seek the Lord! Consider the rock from which you
were cut, the quarry from which you were mined.
Yes, think about Abraham, your ancestor, and
Sarah, who gave birth to your nation. Abraham
was only one man when I called him. But when I
blessed him, he became a great nation."

— ISAIAH 51:1-2

Abraham was one man when God called him, but he became a
mighty nation. Part of your birthright as the seed of
Abraham is that you are a nation in one man or one woman. And
like Abraham, if Jesus tarries, Revival Today will have large
property holdings and own private security. Why? Because as Bible
prophecy unfolds, people and the government will adopt harsher
and harsher stances against churches and God's People.

THE KEY TO DELIVERANCE

Does the Bible say the key to deliverance is to ask someone to pray for you? No! Read Isaiah 51 again: *"...all who hope for deliverance...consider the rock from which you were cut, the quarry from which you were mined. Yes, think about Abraham, your ancestor, and Sarah, who gave birth to your nation. Abraham was only one man when I called him, but when I blessed him, he became a great nation."*

That's the Bible's secret to deliverance: consider your *spiritual* heritage. You are not a struggling Nigerian. You are not a struggling Ghanaian. It's not hard in South Africa. It's not hard for black people. As Christians, the seed of Abraham, everything God promised Abraham belongs to you and to me. We carry the capacity to rule when we look to our spiritual heritage.

> For the sin of this one man, Adam, caused death to
> rule over many. But even greater is God's
> wonderful grace and his gift of righteousness, for
> all who receive it will live in triumph over sin
> and death through this one man, Jesus Christ.
>
> — ROMANS 5:17

The Weymouth Translation puts it this way: *"For if, through the transgression of the one individual, Death made use of the one individual to seize the sovereignty, all the more shall those who receive God's overflowing grace and gift of righteousness reign as kings in Life through the one individual, Jesus Christ."*

Write this down: *Reign as kings in life.* Put that where you will see it every day.

God created Adam as a sovereign king in the earth. *The heavens belong to the Lord, the earth I've given to you.* (Psalm 115:16) *This is your garden. Name it what you want. Do what you want. Just don't touch that one tree, the Tree of Knowledge of Good and Evil, that is set apart for me.* (Genesis 2:17)

But Adam disobeyed, and death (Satan) claimed Adam's kingship. Until Christ came. Now, all those who receive God's overflowing grace and gift of righteousness *reign as kings in Life* through the one individual, Jesus Christ. (Romans 5:17, Weymouth & Amplified)

How does this tie into deliverance? Is it possible to understand this truth and still feel like you always need prayer? Now, if someone wants to pray, "Open doors for Jonathan, and bless Jonathan," I'm all for that. It's the "worry prayers" focused on, "I just need prayer. I just need a break," that I'm talking about.

Adam *was* a king, who lost his sovereignty through sin and death by refusing to obey God (don't touch that one tree) and take dominion. But Christ restored that sovereignty unto man through His death, burial, and resurrection so that we may again reign as kings in *this* life...*if we choose to do so.* I choose dominion through Christ. I don't need people to circle around me and rub my shoulders and pray I get dominion. I *have* dominion. I reign as a king in *this* life. Thank you, Jesus.

What would happen in your world if you chose to be a king?

What if you changed your focus from begging with "worry prayers" and started seeing yourself as a king? Some preachers go so far as to say that's why Christ is called the King of kings. He is the King (capital K) of the small "kings" — us! He's our head, the head King; Making him the King of kings.

51

Of course, many who hear people like me teach this way often respond with, "Oh, he must be a cult. That can't be Christianity." Part of the reason for this response is rooted in how Christians talk down about themselves.

"How many of you know we're nothing? He's everything. How many of you know that we're weak, we make mistakes, and we fail God every day?"

If that's your focus, you'll be at the altar every week needing prayer. Why? You're self-identifying as a chump instead of a king. "I'm nothing. I miss it every day, and I'm sure I displease God a multitude of ways." No! You have been redeemed. You are redeemed. According to Romans 5:17, you are a king.

Say it. *I'm the seed of Abraham.* When kings went to war, they asked Abraham for help. Abraham didn't walk around wringing his hands engaging in "worry talk" or "worry prayer." "Well, I'm just concerned about what our President's doing. Did you hear they're voting to raise taxes, again? How will we afford that?" No. I am a king and I have dominion over the evil that any man may be doing in the earth.

Like my father Abraham, my focus is on the God of my blessing. There is no group of "they" who possess the capacity to do something to me. I am a nation in one man who will leave a deposit on this earth that positively affects my generation and generations to come.

Consider Billy Graham, who was treated like a dignitary. When he died, people flew in from all over the world, kings and ministers of nations. I don't mean preacher ministers; I mean prime ministers. They either came or sent someone, just like when a dignitary dies. Billy Graham also received the honor of being one of only four private citizens to have been laid in State in the Capitol Building. They even drove his body down Billy Graham Parkway in North Carolina, the highway named after him.

John Osteen, father of Joel Osteen, also preached and lived out a life of dominion. What did his choice and his focus produce in his life? He owned the largest arena in Houston, built the largest church in America—and one of the largest churches in the world— at that time. That's what his choice produced and continues to produce through his son Joel.

Never fall into the trap that taking dominion is theory. We see it clearly spelled out in the Bible. We have witnessed its power repeat through history, both past and present. You are the seed of Abraham. Dominion is yours. **But it only works if you work it.** Do you see yourself as a struggling chump trying to serve God? Or have you put that chump to death and declared you are redeemed, brought back to life through Christ, to reign as a King in *this* life?

Much of what happens next in your life will be driven by which one you choose. If you choose king, dress like one. I'm not talking about having designer clothes plastered all over you like a NASCAR driver to let people know you have expensive taste. In the words of Bishop Oyedepo, "it's not your clothes that make you look poor; it's your care for those clothes that make you look poor." Carry yourself with class and dignity. Stand up straight. Stop using your mouth to put yourself down.

Jesus said you are *the salt of the earth*. (Matthew 5:13). You are *the light of the world*. (Matthew 5:14) You are hooked up with Christ.

The Apostle Paul wrote…

For to me to live is Christ, and to die is gain.

— PHILIPPIANS 1:12 (NIV)

Yes, you could check out and go live happily-ever-after in Glory. But that's not your purpose. You are here, on this earth, as an ambassador of Heaven, a foreign dignitary from the Kingdom, here to give. Yes, *give*. Not receive.

> But my God shall supply all your need according to
> his riches in glory by Christ Jesus.

— PHILIPPIANS 4:19 (KJV)

God is fulfilling all your needs according to His riches in glory by Christ Jesus. You don't need the world. The world needs you.

Some people hear that and think, "now, that's arrogance."

And it would be if I were here to lord my position over you, and the world.

Here's what Jesus had to say about those who did (and do) just that.

"Watch out! Don't do your good deeds publicly, to be admired by others, for you will *lose the reward* [emphasis mine] from your Father in Heaven.

> "When you give to someone in need, don't do as the
>   hypocrites do—blowing trumpets in the
>   synagogues and streets [posting all over social
>   media] to call attention to their acts of charity! I
>   tell you the truth, they have received all the
>   reward they will ever get.
> But when you give to someone in need, don't let

your left hand know what your right hand is
doing.
Give your gifts in private, and your Father, who sees
everything, will reward you."

— MATTHEW 6:1-4

To whom was Jesus pointing his finger when he said this? The religious people of His day, the Sanhedrin—the Pharisees and Sadducees—the teachers of the law?

"Lose their reward? Receive all they will ever get? How dare a filthy uneducated Nazarene from the no-account town make such claims about us." They got so mad, they tried to kill him…and failed.

I'm here to tell you, to remind you, what those religious leaders and most of today's religious leaders will never tell you, straight out.

"And he [Jesus] said unto them [the Pharisees], Ye are from beneath; I am from above: ye are of this world; I am not of this world."

Like Jesus, I am from above, a king. Once dead in sin, He quickened me with Christ, raised me up to sit together in the heavily places with Him. (Ephesians 2:5-6)

You can have the same if you choose to.

For by grace are ye saved through faith; and that not
of yourselves: it is the gift of God:
Not of works, lest any man should boast.
For we are his workmanship, created in Christ Jesus

unto good works, which God hath before
ordained that we should walk in them.
Wherefore remember, that ye being in time past
    Gentiles in the flesh, who are called
    Uncircumcision by that which is called the
    Circumcision in the flesh made by hands;
That at that time ye were without Christ, being aliens
    from the commonwealth of Israel, and strangers
    from the covenants of promise, having no hope,
    and without God in the world:
But now in Christ Jesus ye who sometimes were far
    off are made nigh by the blood of Christ.
You, too, can be from above, a king. Once dead in
    sin, you too can be quickened with Christ, raised
    to sit together with Him heavily places.

— EPHESIANS 2:5-6 (KJV)

But it only works when you put aside your human "roots"—your ethnic background—and consider the rock from which you were cut" and work it.

BREAKING INTO YOUR BEST DESTINY

Step 1: Break With Your Father's Family

Allow me to say, from the start, I am talking about the family you grew up in. NOT your spouse. NOT your children.

Many Christians never receive the best of God because their family (the one they grew up in) has no regard, or a light regard, for God and His blessings.

Remember, you cannot continue to identify with your earthly roots *and* receive what's of heaven.

If you grew up in a godly family like mine, then the break will likely be a smaller degree and possibly more difficult. If you grew up in a family that doesn't have much regard for God and His Word, then the break will come at a larger degree, and could be much easier.

But everybody, to some degree, must break with their earthly father, and their earthly roots to enter their Abrahamic destiny.

Again, I want to be very clear. I'm *not* talking about your spouse or kids. I'm talking about the family in which you grew up.

I also want to address "church families." This may make me a few more enemies, but it needs to be said. There's a problem when a church is called the Spanish Pentecostal church, or the Black Pentecostal church, or the White Pentecostal church.

Break ties with any community that insists on identifying itself by its early heritage. Why? You cannot identify with this earth *and* receive what's of heaven.

Let's return to Genesis 12 in the New Living Translation and take another look at what God has to say about breaking family ties.

> The Lord had said to Abram, "Leave your native country, your relatives, and your father's family, and go to the land that I will show you."
>
> — GENESIS 12:1

Notice the command: *break ties* with all that is familiar and go to a place you know nothing about.

> "I will make you into a great nation. I will bless you and make you famous, and you will be a blessing to others. I will bless those who bless you and curse those who treat you with contempt. All the families on earth will be blessed through you."
> So, Abram departed as the Lord had instructed, and Lot went with him. Abram was seventy-five years old when he left Haran. He took his wife, Sarai, his nephew Lot, and all his wealth—his livestock and all the people he had taken into his household at Haran—and headed for the land of Canaan.
>
> — GENESIS 12: 2-5

I don't imagine Abraham's father was incredibly happy about his son's "financial withdraw" of his contribution to the family "dynasty," do you?

When they arrived in Canaan, Abram traveled

through the land as far as Shechem. There he set
up camp beside the oak of Moreh. At that time,
the area was inhabited by Canaanites.
Then the Lord appeared to Abram and said, "I will
give this land to your descendants." And Abram
built an altar there and dedicated it to the Lord,
who had appeared to him.

— GENESIS 12:5-7

Remember, anybody God ever made a covenant with, He turned
land over to them.

After that Abraham traveled South, and set up camp
in the hill country with Bethel to the West, and
Ai to the East. There he built another altar and
dedicated it to the Lord, and he worshiped the
Lord. Then Abraham continued traveling South
by stages toward the Negev.

— GENESIS 12: 8-9

What's the first thing Abraham had to do to dominate in a wicked
nation? Get up and leave his "stomping grounds," leave his
relatives, endure all the arguments, all the pleading, all the tears, all
the "but you said you would..." guilt trips, and follow God's
leading.

Now, if you are honest with yourself, how much does your mom or
dad care about and support you when it comes to the things of God?
If your answer is hardly or not at all, your path is clear: part ways
and go in a different direction. But what can be more of a handicap

is if your parents are lukewarm Christians with a half-hearted or light-regard for faith, for the baptism of the Holy Ghost, for healing, for tithing, for prosperity.

"Oh, there's that faith message again. Kenneth Hagin. Yeah, I knew a guy who went to RHEMA. Look at him now. You don't want to end up like that, now, do you?"

Yet, they've attended a full-gospel church for 30-35 years and somehow remained the same.

Why does this matter? Because the Bible says...

> "Blessed are those who hunger and thirst for
> righteousness, for they will be filled."
>
> — MATTHEW 5:6 (NIV)

If there is no infilling, there is no hunger or thirst for righteousness.

And what was the one thing God counted toward Abraham?

> In the same way, Abraham believed God, and God
> counted him as righteous because of his faith.
>
> — GALATIANS 3:6

The real children of Abraham, then, are those who put their faith in God.

These are hard words. But, this is a truth that must be addressed if you and your immediate family (spouse and children) are to break into God's best.

When I was six years old, I was baptized in the Holy Ghost, because *I* wanted it.

If I'd consulted with, or confided in, the counselor at the kid's church camp, or even with a pastor of today's many so-called full-gospel churches, I would have likely heard, "That's great little Johnny, but I don't think so. That's more for adults. Peter was an adult. You actually don't see any kids in the Bible baptized in the Holy Ghost. So, I don't even know if it's scriptural."

And yet, even at the age of six, I knew what had happened.

Many of you have experienced this same frustration. You've heard me and others teach on healing, prosperity, tithing, the power of the Holy Ghost, and it excited your spirit. You shared it with your family thinking they would share your excitement, and they not only didn't care, but they also didn't like it and then tried to talk you out of it.

Yet they never tried talking you out of drinking or partying, but they tried to talk you out of tithing while still calling themselves Christians.

The encouragement here is, there's not one single recording of Abraham's father saying, "Oh, let me come with you, son. This sounds like a great plan."

If your family is normal, they want you to do well—to a point, and on their terms. But when you start going past where they've gone, or where they think you should go, they'll go from supporting you to attempting to pull you back in line with their expectations.

So, how do you honor your parents, as the Bible directs (Ephesians 6:2) when they maintain a light-regard for the things of God? It's an important question that starts with understanding that honoring someone has nothing to do with allowing that person to control your life. There's a reason why Genesis 2:24 says, *"Therefore shall a man leave his father and his mother, and shall cleave unto his wife: and they shall be one flesh."*

If you find yourself saying, "Well, we would come to this church on a regular basis, but my parents really want us in their church so we can go out to dinner afterward and they can see more of the grandkids…" —You've now shelved any expectation of receiving God's best.

When Abraham left his father's house, there's no record of him asking permission. For that matter, Abraham never even consulted his wife. So, if Sarah is your root as a godly woman, and you find yourself thinking, "Well, I know God told Abraham we're to depart for points unknown, but I told him, as soon as God speaks to me, then we'll go," then you're not of Sarah. You're not of Abraham's lineage. The Lord speaks to the leader, and the man.

Now, you needn't have a big blow-out with your mother or father or your spouses' parents. But you do have to go where the Lord is directing and refuse to allow anyone to override it. Using hindsight, imagine how insane it would have been if Abraham had replied back to God, "ya know, I talked to dad, and he has these plans that we've been working on, and he's not going to be around for too many more years, so what if we found a way to…"

Here's what Jesus had to say about such…

> For I am come to set a man at variance against his
> father, and the daughter against her mother, and
> the daughter in law against her mother in law.
> And a man's foes shall be they of his own household.
> He that loveth father or mother more than me is not

worthy of me: and he that loveth son or daughter
more than me is not worthy of me.

— MATTHEW 10:35-37 (KJV)

If you're going to do what Abraham did, have what he had, be
blessed the way he was blessed, become a mighty nation in one man
or woman inside of your own lifetime, you're going to have to
conquer the enemies in your own family (remember, the one you
grew up in). This is where most Christians miss it.

If a homeless guy on the street, who was demon-possessed, told
you, "I don't want you going to that church. You're never going to
make it. That pastor is a false prophet." You would just say, "Oh,
that's a demon talking."

Now, from your mother or father—who never attended church a day
in their lives, and have no opinions about healing, or the baptism of
the Holy Ghost or tithing—you might actually get, "Hey, whatever.
That's your thing…knock yourself out."

But if you face a lukewarm family with just enough religion to
make them dangerous, and you start moving forward in God, your
actions will expose their lukewarmness. Most people, rather than
change and follow your lead, will just get mad at you for doing
what they haven't the courage to do: Believe God, step out of their
comfort zone, and into faith.

In the words of Elijah…

How long halt ye between two opinions? if the Lord
be God, follow him: but if Baal, then follow him.

— I KINGS 18:21 (KJV)

"Okay. Maybe if I back off the blessing 'stuff' to an acceptable level, keeping most of it to myself, my family won't get so upset, and they'll stop thinking I'm crazy."

I want you to hear this. Compromise, and you'll recycle all your family's lukewarmness. Even worse, you'll pass it down to your children. Lukewarmness is like a barrier in the spirit realm, a barrier your family has never crossed. You can either stay back behind it too, or you can push forward like Abraham, saying, "I'm breaking through. I'm taking new ground."

Most Christians never receive the best of God because they refuse to break with the family in which they grew up and other communities with no regard or a light regard for God and his blessings.

Don't be one of them. Instead, "consider the rock from which you were hewn."

Step 2: Identify What You Are Breaking From

An interesting fact about Abraham's dad: He was an idol worshiper.

> "This is what the Lord, the God of Israel, says:
> 'Long ago your ancestors, including Terah the
> father of Abraham and Nahor, lived beyond the
> Euphrates River and worshiped other gods.'"
>
> — JOSHUA 24:2

According to Jewish tradition, Abraham's father, Terah, was also an idol maker. To continue living in his father's house, God knew Abraham would need to continue to tolerate both. We also know how God feels about any god or idol that comes before Him.

I am the Lord thy God, which have brought thee out
    of the land of Egypt, out of the house of bondage.
Thou shalt have no other gods before me.
Thou shalt not make unto thee any graven image, or
    any likeness of any thing that is in heaven above,
    or that is in the earth beneath, or that is in the
    water under the earth.
Thou shalt not bow down thyself to them, nor serve
    them: for I the Lord thy God am a jealous God,
    visiting the iniquity of the fathers upon the
    children unto the third and fourth generation of
    them that hate me;
And shewing mercy unto thousands of them that love
    me, and keep my commandments.

— EXODUS 20:2-6 (KJV)

What does your family tolerate? Alcoholism? Sexual immorality? Backbiting? Gossip? Lying? Cheating? Sowing discord? Bowing to other gods? (More sleep, less church. More time watching football, playing golf, kids sports rather than gathering yourselves together.)

You can't tolerate what God abhors and go to where God has called you to be.

If you are an adult still living in your father's house, break from your family, make God's calling your priority.

If you've formed a family of your own, examine what you're tolerating, including any influence your mom and dad or other communities have on your decisions. The family you grew up in didn't become lukewarm by accident. Neither will yours. Here's a good way to know if you've successfully cleared your house...

If Kenneth Hagin or Billy Graham showed up at your door, what would you apologize for as they walked through your house? "Oh, that's the door to our wine cellar. We almost never drink wine; it's just a thing we collect." "Yes, I know that painting shows the woman's breasts. It's actually a classic from Spain." "Yes, my son studies horror flicks. He's a film student at... It's a required curriculum." Anything you feel compelled to apologize for, remove.

Step 3: Not Everyone Will Come Along For The Ride

If you think you're going to go forward with God, and bring all your friends and family members and they're all going to skip with you down the golden brick road to the wonderful land of Oz—it ain't happening. Abraham's life proved it. Jesus' life did too.

> Jesus left that part of the country and returned with
> his disciples to Nazareth, his hometown. The
> next Sabbath he began teaching in the
> synagogue, and many who heard him were
> amazed.
>
> — MARK 6:1-2

But it wasn't the right kind of amazed. It was like, offended amazed.

> They asked, "Where did he get all this wisdom and
> the power to perform such miracles?" Then they
> scoffed, "He's just a carpenter, the son of Mary
> and the brother of James, Joseph, Judas, and
> Simon. And his sisters live right here among us."
> They were deeply offended and refused to
> believe in him.
> Then Jesus told them, "A prophet is honored

everywhere except in his own hometown and among his relatives and his own family. "And because of their unbelief, he couldn't do any miracles among them except to place his hands on a few sick people and heal them. And he was amazed at their unbelief.

— MARK 6: 2-6

If Jesus couldn't get his family to honor him, what makes you think you can get your family to honor you?

The more people know you personally, the less they receive from you. That's why mighty men of God who have impacted the world, it is their own children who are the least impacted; they never received one ounce of impartation from the dad.

It'd be like walking with Jesus for three and a half years, and when asked what stood out to you about the life of Christ, you said, "Well, he loved riding in boats. Sleeping in them too. Oh, and he loved eating fish." Your family is the last who will receive you.

You can beat yourself up over that. Ponder, "Man, what could I have done differently?" Ask yourself this, instead. Did Jesus do something wrong that led to Judas being like he was? Did God do something wrong that caused Adam and Eve to turn and disobey him? Did God do something wrong that caused Lucifer to take a third of the angels and leave heaven? Did Jesus do something wrong to his family, to the town, and that's why they wouldn't receive him?

Many Christians think if they bring someone close to them, they can change them. But you can't turn a wolf into a sheep.

Jesus laid out the truth and allowed people the freedom to choose which of the four grounds—stony, thorny, the wayside, or fertile—they wanted to be. (Matthew 13:1-23, Parable of the Sower)

I don't hire anybody in this ministry as a reclamation project. "Jonathan, my son has been on and off drugs. I just really feel like if he could get around your ministry, it would help him." Yeah, maybe —not a roll of the dice I'm willing to make.

Jesus was careful who he brought close to him. I'll minister to anybody, but I'm not bringing them into my home. "We do a homeless outreach. And we met a guy, he's a great guy. He was homeless. So, we brought him in to live with our family." Mistake. If the Holy Spirit can't change someone's heart from stony to fertile ground, I'm not going to have better success.

You can do everything right and have anybody go down the wrong path.

God lost Adam and Eve. *God* lost Adam and Eve. They turned on him. They disobeyed him. What did He do wrong? Should've made the garden of Eden nicer? Shouldn't have cut so many corners? Jesus' family wouldn't receive him. What did he do wrong?

Stop beating yourself up. Every man is 100% responsible for the outcome of his own life. God's not responsible. The Devil's too small to blame—other people aren't responsible.

I will give an account for what I did or didn't do with my life. Nobody else. "Oh, I'm just a messed-up human waiting on God. He'll turn me around someday." No, you are playing the part of the slothful servant who buried the one talent the Master gave him, instead of putting it to use.

Here was the outcome of that choice…

"Then the servant with the one bag of silver came
and said, 'Master, I knew you were a harsh man,
harvesting crops you didn't plant and gathering
crops you didn't cultivate. I was afraid I would
lose your money, so I hid it in the earth. Look,
here is your money back.'
But the master replied, 'You wicked and lazy
servant! If you knew I harvested crops I didn't
plant and gathered crops I didn't cultivate, why
didn't you deposit my money in the bank? At
least I could have gotten some interest on it.'
Then he ordered, 'Take the money from this servant,
and give it to the one with the ten bags of silver.
To those who use well what they are given, even
more will be given, and they will have an
abundance. But from those who do nothing, even
what little they have will be taken away. Now
throw this useless servant into outer darkness,
where there will be weeping and gnashing of
teeth.'"

— MATTHEW 25:24-30

The intelligent man examines himself, and his actions, daily and
knows that not everyone will come along for the ride.

Step 4: Move Beyond What Others Think

90% of the stress in life is caused by focusing on the actions and approval of others. Write that down. Put it someplace where you will see it *every* day. 90% of life's stress comes when you seek the approval of others.

If you know it's the right path, and you have God's approval, focus and move forward. Refuse to put your happiness in the hands of someone else's emotions. "I just wish my mom could see my husband the way I see him. She would like him." Who cares whether she likes him or not? Who's she? Thoughts like this make you ripe for manipulation.

For some of you—I'm talking to the adults here, not fifteen-year-olds—all your mother has to do is give you "that look" and you're back on her hook. "I could tell that she didn't like that." You're right. She didn't. Now, what's your next move?

Abraham did not subject his decisions to his idol worshiping father's approval. When the Lord said "go," he departed. He didn't run it by his wife. Didn't run it by his mom. Didn't run it by his dad. Didn't run it by his cousins. He moved forward.

Want to know my secret to being almost problematically relaxed? I am completely divorced from allowing the approval or actions of others to affect my daily happiness.

Some time back, a friend of mine, who relapsed back into heroin, texted me around 2am. "I need help." I said, "I'll have someone call you in the morning and get you set up." I had previously offered him a place to live, and he turned it down to live with a friend who had just kicked him out. "I need help," he texted again. I said back, "Your problem is not my emergency. I'm going to sleep. I have a broadcast in the morning."

After 40 years of testing things out, I know the value of a sleepless night, and the grown man on the other end of that text had already rejected my help once. "I'll deal with you in the morning." He said, "Well, where am I supposed to sleep tonight?" I wrote back, "Any flat surface." I'm not going to be much help to anybody if I allow the devil to send one troubled person my way every night and rob me of my sleep.

Luke chapter 2 shows us that Jesus dealt with Lazarus when he was good and ready, ignoring the people who were ticked off because He didn't arrive on their timetable.

"Jesus is taking the time to heal strangers while his so-called friend, Lazarus, is here dying, and he's only a day's walk away. Doesn't sound very Christ-like to me. He's supposed to be the Messiah?" That's how people are. Yet, Jesus never budged. Neither did He spend the next 30 nights crying Himself to sleep because "they" were mad at Him. He moved forward. Went to another place, kept teaching the word, kept *about His Father's business.* (Luke 2:29)

When you're rejected by people, let them reject you. Keep moving forward. If Jesus couldn't bring his family along for the ride, and again, I'm not talking about your spouse and kids; you should always bring them along for the ride. But if Jesus couldn't bring his mother, father, sisters, brothers, his friends from his town, his cousins along, I'll ask you again, what makes you think you can?

In the end, even John the Baptist, Jesus' closest family member, the one who prophesied Jesus was the Messiah, asked, *"Are you the Messiah? Should we look for another?"* (Matthew 11:2). Do not allow people's opinions or their expectations direct your paths. When faced with a choice, you, the seed of Abraham, know the right decision.

> He has told you, O man, what is good; and what does
> the LORD require of you but to do justice, and to
> love kindness, and to walk humbly with
> your God?

— MICAH 6:8 (ESV)

Never allow some schmuck and his opinion or turned-up face cause you to question God's direction. God told Jeremiah...

> Be not afraid of their faces: for I am with thee to
> deliver thee...

— JEREMIAH 1:8 (KJV)

"Brother Jonathan, I know you like to preach on healing. There's some people in our church...they don't really believe in healing." That's why they need to hear it. You don't preach based on what people like. "We're not really going to talk about homosexuality anymore or marriage or genders or heaven and hell or Christ being the only way to heaven is kind of offense." Respond to God's call and move beyond what others think.

Step 5: Sometimes You Must Go Alone

> And Abraham said unto his young men, Abide ye
> here with the ass; and I and the lad [Isaac] will
> go yonder and worship, and come again to you.

— GENESIS 22:5 (KJV)

If you're going to do what Abraham did and get what Abraham got, then you're going to have to follow Abraham's path. Sometimes you have to go alone. Write this down. Put it where you will read it every day: *if you walk, you walk with many. If you run, you run with few. If you fly, you fly alone.*

If you're going to go to where God called you to go, there's going to be people you must leave back with the asses. Yes, you can take it both ways.

Step 6: God Will Give You A New Family

Joshua reminds the tribes of Israel...

> "This is what the Lord, the God of Israel, says: Long
> ago your ancestors, including Terah, the father of
> Abraham and Nahor, lived beyond the Euphrates
> River, and they worshiped other gods. But I took
> your ancestor Abraham from the land beyond the
> Euphrates and led him into the land of Canaan. I
> gave him many descendants through his son
> Isaac."

> — JOSHUA 24:2-3

Then Joshua calls the Israelites to choose...

> "So fear the Lord and serve him wholeheartedly. Put
> away forever the idols your ancestors worshiped
> when they lived beyond the Euphrates River and
> in Egypt. Serve the Lord alone.
> But if you refuse to serve the Lord, then choose
> today whom you will serve. Would you prefer the

gods your ancestors served beyond the
Euphrates? Or will it be the gods of the Amorites
in whose land you now live? But as for me and
my family, we will serve the Lord."

— JOSHUA 24:14-15

Are you going to stay where your family's been your entire life, allowing them to fence you in, too? Or are you going to break free and move forward into God's greater blessings? If your choice is to break free (not of just one or two things, but of everything that can so easily beset) and move forward, then you know what needs to be done.

You know what needs to be removed from your life. You know whose opinions dominate your decision-making, and you know how to stop them. You know who is manipulating you and how to stop their influence.

Do what the Word says; follow His voice with your whole heart and do it with abandon.

Therefore, since we are surrounded by such a huge
crowd of witnesses to the life of faith, let us strip
off every weight that slows us down, especially
the sin that so easily trips us up. And let us run
with endurance the race God has set before us.
We do this by keeping our eyes on Jesus, the
champion who initiates and perfects our faith.

— HEBREWS 12:1-2

BONUS CONTENT: HESITANT WIFE + CONFUSED KIDS
= CHANGING YOU

"What if it causes a divorce?" That's not possible based on what I taught. I mentioned many times, this is not your wife or your husband or your kids. This is about outside family. Once you got married, you entered into a covenant till death do us part. A man who abandons his family is worse than an infidel. That's what the Bible says. So don't be stupid.

It only works when you put aside your human "roots"—your ethnic background—and "consider the rock from which you were cut" and work it.

> So, Abram departed as the Lord had instructed, and
> Lot went with him. Abram was seventy-five
> years old when he left Haran. He took his wife,
> Sarai, his nephew Lot, and all his wealth—his
> livestock and all the people he had taken into his
> household at Haran—and headed for the land of
> Canaan.
>
> — GENESIS 12:4-5

If you're going do what Abraham did, have what he had, be blessed the way he was blessed, become a mighty nation in one man or woman inside of your own lifetime, you're going to have to conquer the enemies in your own household, first.

The intelligent man examines himself and his actions daily and knows that not everyone will come along for the ride.

Respond to God's call and move beyond what others think.

LESSON 5

YOU CAN'T BE A BEGGAR AND A KING

Many believers have traded in their place of kingly dominion to beg.

The Bible says we have all been made priests of God, that Christ, the firstborn of many brethren and who is a King, has made us kings on this earth *to reign as kings in this life* (Romans 5:17).

We can't be a king and a beggar at the same time. You must make a choice.

It's not your clothes that make you a beggar; it's the act of begging that makes you a beggar. Many ministers are well-dressed beggars.

If you choose to beg, you'll never enter into the blessing of your Abrahamic covenant. If your Cash App or PayPal is in your bio on social media, you'll never enter into the blessing of God. If you're always looking for help, you can't be like Abraham, and you can't be like Jesus. You have to make a decision today, whether you'll be a king or a beggar.

I could be friends with somebody for years, but if they send me a private text message asking for money for their ministry, I usually block the number, especially if they are someone that preaches prosperity out of the word of God.

There's nothing wrong with asking people for prayer—but I don't even do that. I want to challenge you to make today the last day you ever say the words "I need...."

> But my God shall supply all your need according to
> his riches in glory by Christ Jesus.
>
> — PHILIPPIANS 4:19 (KJV)

That does not necessitate my making people aware of my needs.

> The LORD is my shepherd;
> I have all that I need.
>
> — PSALM 23:1

It's not a sin to borrow, but it's *anti-covenant* to borrow. Borrowing implies there is an unmet need. The Bible says when the Lord is your shepherd, you won't lack anything. Abraham's storehouse was filled with grain. Before the need arose, the provision was there ahead of time.

We don't ask people to help us raise money for a project in our ministry. We just announce that we've bought a building or begun a project. All I ask you to do is to give as you're directed by the Spirit. Now, anytime we make a move, the money is there beforehand. That is how Abraham operated, and that's how the blessing of God works. *The Lord is my shepherd; I shall not want.*

When I hear somebody begging, I know there's a problem. People have creative ways of begging. If someone is asking on Facebook *how* to hire a moving truck, that's begging. Do you know *how* to get a moving truck? Google it and then follow the stream from there. When people ask, "Does anyone know where I can get a couch?" It's just an online way of sitting on the sidewalk with an empty coffee cup, asking for change.

You have two eyes in your head. Can you make one look up at the sky and one look down at the ground simultaneously? No, not without tearing a retina. Neither can you claim to be trusting God while looking to people for help. You're not going to see Abraham making people aware of his needs and asking if they can help.

If you trade in your place of kingly dominion to beg, you'll never prosper. If there's a need, tell the Lord.

BE A GIVER, NOT A BEGGAR

A beggar can never enter into Abrahamic dominion and prosperity.

When the king of Sodom wanted to give Abraham money, he said, *"I won't take so much as a shoe latchet from you. It allows you to say you made me rich. But only God is going to be able to say He made me rich."*

It's anti-covenant to demand favor from somebody. You decrease favor by doing so because it decreases a person's desire to give you anything in the future.

Jesus didn't beg. You will never find Jesus Christ begging. When Jesus was in the wilderness, He never said, "I've been here for a long time. Does anybody have any bread or fish I can eat?"

Jesus didn't hoard. God is a provider, and if you lose sight of that truth, you'll hoard. When someone gave Jesus and the disciples bread and fish, He didn't tell the disciples, "Don't let anybody know we have this. That way, we can eat the five loaves and the two fish among us. I know it's not much, but that way, at least, we won't starve."

That's why I don't agree with anyone who prophesies that there will be a food shortage. Show me somewhere in the Bible where God's people lacked food. God caused manna to rain down in the wilderness. When they got sick of manna, he gave them so much quail that they vomited it up.

Jesus provided. He took the five loaves and two fish, had everybody sit down in groups of 50 and 100, gave thanks for it, blessed it, and multiplied it out to the people until everybody ate, until full.

If you're going to be like Abraham, and you're going to be like Christ, you cannot have a begging or hoarding mentality. You must have a giving mentality.

Not only do I never have to worry about having enough, but the Lord will also make my cup run over so I can supply those who are hurting around me.

> The LORD appeared again to Abraham near the oak
> grove belonging to Mamre. One day Abraham
> was sitting at the entrance to his tent during the
> hottest part of the day. He looked up and noticed
> three men standing nearby. When he saw them,
> he ran to meet them and welcomed them, bowing
> low to the ground.
> "My lord," he said, "if it pleases you, stop here for a
> while. Rest in the shade of this tree while water

is brought to wash your feet. And since you've
honored your servant with this visit, let me
prepare some food to refresh you before you
continue on your journey."

— GENESIS 18:1-5

Abraham was like an Italian. When I preached at a church in
Montreal, a lady named Angie Dividio invited me to stay in their
family's home. They were from Italy. The husband worked all day,
and the wife tended to the house and raised their son. I was about
two years out of Bible college. Until that moment, I had never been
treated as well as she treated me.

She cooked all the traditional Italian dishes. Every meal, she would
lay out a whole spread. Every time I thought, "How in the world am
I going to eat all this food?" If I didn't eat enough, she'd get upset
and say, "I have noticed you haven't eaten any of this. Have some."
So, I ate way more than I wanted to eat. Then, she'd clear the table
and bring a second course, usually steak.

At the time, I was preaching for the young adults, and afterward, I
and all the youth would go out. By the time I returned to her home
each night, it was almost two in the morning, and I was just going to
go straight to bed. But each time, she had a full dinner waiting for
me. When I woke up in the morning, she had fresh fruit for
breakfast, espresso, and scrambled eggs adorned with an Italian flag
on top.

She noticed my suits were way too big for me, so she took me to a
tailor and got me measured. She bought a black suit from a place
called Signor Terry's in Montreal. She purchased many more things
for me. I was treated like a king.

Angie was a former Catholic before she was saved. She said, "The Bible says that whatever you do to the least of these, you're doing it unto me, and to treat people that minister the word of God like you would treat Jesus. So, I'm doing for you what I would do if Jesus was staying in my home." She was not exaggerating!

There's no way you could have treated a human being better than she treated me in her home. These were not rich people. These were just Abrahamic people, the Jesus type of people. They were common people that acted like Abraham. They did not ask me if I could help them, either.

In Genesis 18:2 Abraham said, *"I won't let you go until you let me feed you."* When I read that story, I think of Angie Davidio.

Jesus provided. Abraham provided.

> Jesus said to them, "If you are Abraham's children, do the deeds of Abraham."
>
> — JOHN 8:39 (NASB)

ABRAHAM LOOKED FOR WHO TO BLESS

Abraham was not looking for someone to help him. Abraham was not looking for who could bless him. Abraham was looking for who to bless.

Two summers ago, I met a multimillionaire preacher. I didn't go there hoping that he'd give me some money for my ministry. I brought *him* money and sowed it to him. Why? If I make that happen for him in his older years, it stores up a harvest for someone to bless me when I'm in my later years, and the Lord will bless me.

He remarks about it all the time publicly, "You're one of three preachers I've ever had come to my home that didn't ask me for money, and actually came and brought money." That's what Abraham did.

Whenever you're looking for someone who can help you, you're out of alignment with the Abrahamic blessing.

You must look for who you can bless as directed by the Spirit, not just throwing money around to whoever's in need. There's an old saying: "If you have six poor people and one rich person, very soon, you'll have seven poor people." Because if all you do is help everywhere there's a need, it's a trap, and it will suck you dry. Let each man give as he's directed by the Spirit.

Every time you look for who to bless, you're coming into alignment with Jesus and Abraham.

> "I have no complaint about your sacrifices or the
> burnt offerings you constantly offer.
> But I do not need the bulls from your barns or the
> goats from your pens.
> For all the animals of the forest are mine, and I own
> the cattle on a thousand hills.
> I know every bird on the mountains, and all the
> animals of the field are mine.
> If I were hungry, I would not tell you, for all the
> world is mine and everything in it."
>
> — PSALM 50:8-12

That's God's mentality—"Everything belongs to Me." So, if everything belongs to God, and you are God's child, everything that belongs to Him belongs to you. The wealth and riches of this world are under the dominion of the children of God.

Just like God said, if I was hungry, I wouldn't ask you for food. Whatever thing you see as a need, you don't look outside. You understand that you have access to it because it belongs to God, and you belong to God.

The last time you ever started a sentence with "I need..." let it be the last time you ever do it.

Frequently I don't have a pen, or I run out of gum. Because I've been meditating on this, I've had to break this habit. "I need gum. I need a pen."—I won't say it.

I'd rather just be rude and say, "Give me your pen," than "I need a pen."

Isn't that what Jesus did with the donkey?

> "Go into that village over there," he told them. "As soon as you enter it, you will see a young donkey tied there that no one has ever ridden. Untie it and bring it here. If anyone asks, 'What are you doing?' just say, 'The Lord needs it and will return it soon.'"
>
> — MARK 11:2-3

Jesus did not send out a letter to His partner saying, "I need a donkey. Can anyone help us raise money for a donkey?"

Don't say it. Break the habit.

All things are God's, and I belong to Him. So, indirectly, all things are in my possession.

> ...We own nothing, and yet we have everything.
>
> — 2 CORINTHIANS 6:10 (NIV)

That is because we're stewarding it for the Lord. That's why the Lord will speak to you at any given time to let something go. It shows that you're in that relationship.

"I want you to give that to him."

"But that's mine, Lord."

"Oh, I thought you were stewarding what I own. Okay. Well, now that it's yours, knock yourself out, live your own little life."

The Lord will do that to test you or check you. If you own nothing, then you're willing to let anything go. I had the Lord speak to me to give my Cadillac Escalade to somebody. It was paid off, and I just gave it to a pastor. When you show the Lord that you can walk away from anything He gives you, He'll never stop letting things come through your hands.

"We own nothing, and yet we have everything."

You steward and multiply something because you know it belongs to the Lord, and you're a faithful servant. But when it comes time to let it pass through your hands to where the master wants it to go, you let it go. Then, God releases more into your care.

Everything God gives you ultimately belongs to Him, including people. You'll hear ministers get upset, "He had my people at his meeting." They're not your people. They're God's people. They might attend your church, and the Lord entrusted them to your pasture, but you're not Jim Jones. You don't own the people.

"I hope the government passes the stimulus because then we can get $2,000." You're brain dead. I don't even think you know the value of $2,000. It's not going to do anything for you.

I don't want any money from the government, just like Abraham didn't take any from the King of Sodom.

People who accepted free housing from the government are now the government's servants. They have to vote a certain way and compromise on everything the Bible says so they can get their money from Lucifer and keep their government housing and their government money.

Don't do it. Stop begging. Whoever you allow to become your source, you become their servant. So, if you allow God to be your source, you become His servant, which is wonderful. Learn to hook up with God and let Him be your source. In doing that, you become the true seed of Abraham.

TRUE PROSPERITY CELEBRATES WHAT IT GIVES

If the Lord uses me to provide others with food, how can I ever run out of food myself? God is not looking to meet my needs; God is looking to empower me supernaturally to meet the needs of my generation.

Prosperity is not God meeting your needs. Prosperity is God raising you up to meet the needs of a hurting world. The Lord will use you to do that if you follow these instructions.

"I will make you into a great nation. I will bless you
and make you famous, and you will be a blessing
to others."

— GENESIS 12:2

Most testimonies shared in the church are in the realm of prosperity. It's somebody testifying as if they have prosperity, but it's not really. If someone buys you tires for your car, because it had bald tires, that's not your prosperity. The person who bought the tires has prosperity.

You getting a Mercedes is not prosperity. You owning the Mercedes dealership is the beginning of prosperity. You paying off a mortgage is not prosperity. You being the one that lends the money is the beginning of prosperity.

To qualify for your free government housing, you can never rise above a certain income level, or they kick you out. Subconsciously people will keep themselves at a low level to stay in their free little house.

But God is not looking to give you a little house and a little income. God is looking to set you high above all the nations of the world.

Our ministry gave away over $831,000 last year to other ministries that we have no control over. We can't take it back if things get tough.

"Praise the Lord! Someone bought a vacation for us." That is great. It's worth telling, but it is not prosperity. True prosperity is being the one that doles out the blessing. It isn't somebody giving you a watch; it's you giving a watch to someone. It's not that someone gave you a car; it's you giving a car to someone else.

It isn't wrong to receive what people give you, but don't confuse that for prosperity because that will actually perpetuate a begging mentality. You start thinking the point of prosperity is that people give you stuff. People will, because the more you give, the more you receive. But you need to keep your focus like Abraham.

Think about it: Abraham is an old man, sitting outside of his tent in the heat of the day. He sees men, and his first thought is, "*I wonder if they've had anything to eat, or if they're thirsty. Let me help them out.*" That's the Abrahamic mentality.

LESSON 6

ABRAHAM WAS A TITHE-BUILT MAN

You can sing about the blessing of Abraham all you want, but until you do the works that Abraham did, you'll never see a drop of what he had in your life.

> After Abram returned from his victory over
> Kedorlaomer and all his allies, the king of
> Sodom went out to meet him in the valley of
> Shaveh (that is, the King's Valley).
> And Melchizedek, the king of Salem and a priest of
> God Most High, brought Abram some bread and
> wine. Melchizedek blessed Abram with this
> blessing:
> "Blessed be Abram by God Most High, Creator of
> heaven and earth.
> And blessed be God Most High, who has defeated
> your enemies for you."
> Then Abram gave Melchizedek a tenth of all the
> goods he had recovered.

The king of Sodom said to Abram, "Give back my
people who were captured. But you may keep for
yourself all the goods you have recovered."

Abram replied to the king of Sodom, "I solemnly
swear to the LORD, God Most High, Creator of
heaven and earth, that I will not take so much as
a single thread or sandal thong from what
belongs to you. Otherwise you might say, 'I am
the one who made Abram rich.' I will accept
only what my young warriors have already
eaten, and I request that you give a fair share of
the goods to my allies—Aner, Eshcol, and
Mamre."

— GENESIS 14:17-24

Then the LORD told him, "I am the LORD who
brought you out of Ur of the Chaldeans to give
you this land as your possession."

But Abram replied, "O Sovereign LORD, how can I
be sure that I will actually possess it?"

The LORD told him, "Bring me a three-year-old
heifer, a three-year-old female goat, a three-year-
old ram, a turtledove, and a young pigeon."

— GENESIS 15:7-9

"I am the LORD, and I do not change. That is why
you descendants of Jacob are not already
destroyed. Ever since the days of your ancestors,
you have scorned my decrees and failed to obey
them. Now return to me, and I will return to
you," says the LORD of Heaven's Armies.

"Should people cheat God? Yet you have
    cheated me!
"But you ask, 'What do you mean? When did we
    ever cheat you?'
"You have cheated me of the tithes and offerings due
    to me. You are under a curse, for your whole
    nation has been cheating me. Bring all the tithes
    into the storehouse so there will be enough food
    in my Temple. If you do," says the LORD of
    Heaven's Armies, "I will open the windows of
    heaven for you. I will pour out a blessing so great
    you won't have enough room to take it in! Try it!
    Put me to the test! Your crops will be abundant,
    for I will guard them from insects and disease.
    Your grapes will not fall from the vine before
    they are ripe," says the LORD of Heaven's
    Armies.

— MALACHI 3:6-11

9 FACTS ABOUT TITHING

1. Tithing Honors A Scriptural Command

There is a blessing for obeying God's word.

In Proverbs 11, the Bible says—*"There's he that keepeth more than he should, and it tendeth to poverty. And there's he that releases more and increases all the more."*

It may not make sense, but it's true. I have lived it. Tithing is not giving God 10% of what's in your hand. It is giving that which He has already entrusted you with to see if you'll return it to Him.

People try to justify not tithing by claiming it was a part of the law and Jesus took us out of the law and into grace.

> This Melchizedek was king of the city of Salem and also a priest of God Most High. When Abraham was returning home after winning a great battle against the kings, Melchizedek met him and blessed him. Then Abraham took a tenth of all he had captured in battle and gave it to Melchizedek. The name Melchizedek means "king of justice," and king of Salem means "king of peace." There is no record of his father or mother or any of his ancestors—no beginning or end to his life. He remains a priest forever, resembling the Son of God.
>
> — HEBREWS 7:1-3

They think the tithe was under the Levitical priesthood, which was fulfilled by Christ. But Abraham tithed to Melchizedek over four hundred years before Levi came on the scene.

The priesthood of Melchizedek is forever. The tithe is a forever principle. Even in the garden of Eden, there was a part of the garden that was set apart to God, that man was not to touch. I'm convinced we'll be tithing in the new Jerusalem, in the new earth, and in the new heaven. There has always been a portion of everything reserved for the Lord. That never changes.

Christ has redeemed us from the curse of the law. The Bible says if you're the seed of Abraham, you will do the works that Abraham did, and Abraham was a tither. Jesus took our sin. He didn't take our tithe.

Tithing is not a tax that God puts on people because we sinned. It's an economic flow God created so the money keeps flowing.

> ...And Melchizedek placed a blessing upon Abraham, the one who had already received the promises of God. And without question, the person who has the power to give a blessing is greater than the one who is blessed.
> The priests who collect tithes are men who die, so Melchizedek is greater than they are, because we are told that he lives on.
>
> — HEBREWS 7:6-8

> But Abram replied, "O Sovereign LORD, what good are all your blessings when I don't even have a son? Since you've given me no children, Eliezer of Damascus, a servant in my household, will inherit all my wealth. You have given me no descendants of my own, so one of my servants will be my heir."
> Then the LORD said to him, "No, your servant will not be your heir, for you will have a son of your own who will be your heir." Then the LORD took Abram outside and said to him, "Look up into the sky and count the stars if you can. That's how many descendants you will have!"
> And Abram believed the LORD, and the LORD counted him as righteous because of his faith.
>
> — GENESIS 15:2-6

God told Abraham, *"Look up at the sky and that's how many descendants I'm going to give you."* Abraham believed those things spoken unto him, despite the impossible-looking circumstances in the natural, and God counted him as righteous because of his faith.

Initially, it doesn't make any sense how you're going to give 10% off the top of what comes into your possession when you can't even make a go of it with 100% of what's coming into your possession. Neither does it make any sense for a 100-year-old man, like Abraham, to have a son with his 90-year-old wife. God knows more than you know; it's a supernatural law you need to acknowledge. His ways are higher than your ways; His thoughts are higher than your thoughts.

I don't understand people who say, "Yeah, but if I tithe. I won't be able to pay my heating bill." Go under the covers so no one can see you and pay your tithe. Put on three hoodies and pay your tithe. If I'm going to rob somebody, God is at the bottom of the list. Not tithing is robbing God.

> And here men that die receive tithes; but there he receiveth them, of whom it is witnessed that he liveth.
>
> — HEBREWS 7:8 (KJV)

Your pastor receives the offering. The ushers receive the offering. But it is simultaneously received as a sacrifice to God in heaven by Christ. Your blessing comes from heaven because it's received in heaven.

You give directed by the Spirit to the Lord. It is received by men here in the kingdom. If you keep that straight, it will change your life.

> In addition, we might even say that these Levites—
> the ones who collect the tithe—paid a tithe to
> Melchizedek when their ancestor Abraham paid a
> tithe to him.
>
> — HEBREWS 7:9

2. The Tithe Is Your Time, Your Treasure, And Your Talent

Your seed is your time, talent, and treasure wrapped up into one. It took the best of your time and talent to produce your income. When you give from your income, you're honoring God with your time, your talent, and your treasure all in one.

It took the best of me to produce my tithe. My tithe is the best of me wrapped into one.

All work is unto the Lord. What you get in exchange for that work, you bring back to God. You're honoring Him in your time and your talent when you give Him your treasure. That's why a seed is so valuable.

Many churches try to let people off the hook in their giving. They say, "Maybe you don't give with your talent. You can give with your treasure. You can give with your time. Amen. You can serve at the church." Some guy is on a three-week rotation working in the sound booth; that's supposedly his tithe because he's giving some of his time in the sound booth.

But when you tithe—think about it—your tithe represents your time, your treasure, and your talent. Something you're good at gave you the ability to produce the money, and it took time to do it. That becomes your treasure. And then, as you give God a portion of that treasure, you're giving God the best of you.

Abraham paid the tithe after he risked his life in battle and fought people in hand-to-hand combat. He immediately went to the high priest of God, Melchizedek, and said, *"This is to let you know that I know it's you. It's not normal for men in their eighties to beat people to death and prevail in hand-to-hand combat. So I honor you for giving me the strength, for protecting me, and giving me victory."* Melchizedek said, *"Blessed be Abram. Blessed be God."* He pronounced that blessing over him, and it kept going from there.

An eight-year-old boy gave me $1,054 of his own money from taking care of his chickens and selling their eggs. He was going to give $100, and then in the service, he told his parents, "I want to give all of it." There's an eight-year-old that sowed $1,054 of his own money. He wanted to sow it. His parents were with him, and they were happy he was sowing it. He said, "If he's using this to win souls, then I want it to go to that." That young man is going places!

Everybody lives on the same planet, Earth, but there are very different people. You've got an eight-year-old that has sown a thousand of a thousand, and you have people with hundreds of thousands that won't write a $100-check for an offering in their whole life.

One time a man walked up to me and said, "I'm a greeter at Walmart." He pulled out a crisp, folded $100 bill that he had under his driver's license in his wallet and said, "This was my Christmas bonus for greeting at Walmart, and I want to give it to you." It wasn't Christmas, so he kept that crisp and folded for months.

That's his best. That was that kid's best. There's a difference between giving and giving your best. Abraham gave his best. God gave us His best. When you release your best into the Kingdom of God, that's when God releases His best. Hallelujah!

Abraham didn't give a cow. Abraham gave Isaac.

"Best" is different for everybody. But there comes a time where you need to take things to a new and higher level. If you want to be like your Father, God and like your father, Abraham, you can't just "chip off" a little of what you have. There must come a point in your life where you give your best.

"Father, this is my best. I only have one of these. I'm not sure I can get one of these back in my lifetime."

That's what Abraham did, and after he offered Isaac, that's when things really took off.

3. Your Tithe Provides Divine Protection And Rebukes The Devourer

> Some time later, the LORD spoke to Abram in a
>   vision and said to him, "Do not be afraid, Abram,
>   for I will protect you, and your reward will be
>   great."
>
> — GENESIS 15:1

The rewards for tithing are protection and great reward. After Abraham tithed, God said to him, *"I will protect you and your reward will be great."*

Is there a curse for taking what belongs to God? Think about it… what happened to Adam and Eve when they ate from the fruit of the tree that was reserved for God? They lost the garden.

Tithing brings protection from the curse. When you meet non-tithers, something is always going wrong. God doesn't curse you for not tithing, but the tithe brings protection from the curse into your life. If you've ever seen both a tithing ministry and a non-tithing ministry, it is obvious.

The Devil would love to steal, kill, and destroy your financial harvest. He is kept at bay by God Himself. Tithers spend no time rebuking Satan. God rebukes Satan for tithers.

> "Should people cheat God? Yet you have
>   cheated me!
> But you ask, 'What do you mean? When did we ever
>   cheat you?'
> You have cheated me of the tithes and offerings due
>   to me. You are under a curse, for your whole
>   nation has been cheating me."
>
> — MALACHI 3:8-9

If you come to our ministry, there's nothing broken. We have three state-of-the-art cameras. If any of those go down, we have a full set of backup cameras, so we never have to go down. No one has ever missed a paycheck or a bonus.

It's difficult to tithe in the beginning when the harvest hasn't come in. But you know it's coming. You must stay conscious of that. Find me ministries that don't tithe, and then find me ministries that do. Whether you like them or not, look at what they're doing. You'll see a tremendous difference in their effectiveness.

Obviously, the enemy attacks tithing. That's why God said, *"Be not weary in well-doing for you will reap a reward if you do not give up and quit."*

4. Tithing Provokes Divine Supply

> "Bring all the tithes into the storehouse so there will be enough food in my Temple. If you do," says the LORD of Heaven's Armies, "I will open the windows of heaven for you. I will pour out a blessing so great you won't have enough room to take it in! Try it! Put me to the test! Your crops will be abundant, for I will guard them from insects and disease. Your grapes will not fall from the vine before they are ripe," says the LORD of Heaven's Armies.
>
> — MALACHI 3:10-11

My tithe separates me from the world's financial systems.

It doesn't matter what the economy is like here on Earth. God can bless me all by Himself.

"Prove me now in the tithe and the offering. See if I won't open the windows of heaven and pour out a blessing that's so great you won't have room enough to take it all in. Try it and let me prove it to you."

If you have faith that one day God is going to have an angel blow a trumpet and cause you to molecularly disappear from the earth, maybe you can have faith that God can give you 100X back on every dollar. To me, that one's a little easier to believe in—and I believe in both!

If you actually believe that when you tithe God will open the windows of heaven and pour you out a blessing that's so great that you'll never have enough room to take it all in, then you won't let anything stop you from tithing.

I want you to notice the magnitude of the blessing God said He would give you if you tithe, you'll actually have a problem having enough room to take it all in.

It took all my faith to purchase our office. Then, I thought we'd stay there for the rest of our lives. But we quickly needed the building across the alley, and now both are full. Now I have a problem; I don't have enough space to handle everything God's bringing into our possession, just like God said. If you take the Bible at face-value, it will literally do what it says it will do.

I had two guys stop me when I was preaching in the South. One man said, "I came to your Business of Ministry conference five years ago. Our business took in $100,000; five years later, we took in just under $2 million." It wasn't a startup business. It wasn't a guy in his early twenties. It was a business that had basically stayed at the same level, and then exploded after he applied the principles of tithing in accordance with God's Word.

The other guy said, "We found you on YouTube and we did what you said out of God's Word, and our business tripled last year." He put a seed in my hand to say thank you.

It works. God's Word is not a lie.

> God is no respecter of persons, but in every nation,
> He accepts those who fear Him and do what is
> right.
>
> — ACTS 10:34

God blesses anybody that obeys His instruction. He has no favorites that can get away with evil. Anyone that disobeys the instruction ends up in the same boat.

"See if I won't open the windows of heaven," has more than one meaning. "Windows" denotes something you look through. God will allow you to peer through His windows and see into His realm of divine ideas.

Our evening broadcast called, "Check the News" was a divine idea. It has totally revolutionized our ministry, even the preaching. Now, I don't have to start on Sunday and build a meeting up through Friday. It's just built from the beginning because of a divine idea that God reserves for tithers.

How did Abraham know there was water under the ground and to dig wells when no one dug wells back then?

Think of this: When there was a drought, Abraham's land wasn't in drought, because he had an underground water supply. And that's what caused him to dominate in a wicked nation—peering through the windows of heaven.

5. Tithing Secures Divine Favor For You And Future Generations

When you read about Abraham and his life, you see divine favor.

> For thou, Lord, wilt bless the righteous; with favour
> wilt thou compass him as with a shield.
>
> — PSALM 5:12 (KJV)

God will put favor around you, like a shield.

When Abraham paid a tithe, it was accounted to Levi. In God's mind, Levi was paying tithes when his great-grandfather paid tithes. You can actually store up favor for your children through tithing.

Your tithe secures divine favor for your children (Isaac), your children's children (Jacob), and your children's children's children (Levi, Joseph).

God credits a blessing to your descendants based on what you do. You can store up a harvest for your children based on your actions now. You can clear the way for your child in the Spirit. That's powerful.

> ...paid a tithe to Melchizedek when their ancestor
> Abraham paid a tithe to him. For although Levi
> wasn't born yet, the seed from which he came
> was in Abraham's body when Melchizedek
> collected the tithe from him.
>
> — HEBREWS 7:9-10

6. Tithing Qualifies You To Own Property And Only Lend, Never Borrow

Tithing qualifies you for supernatural land ownership.

When Abraham finished paying his tithe in Genesis 14, God told him that he'd give Abraham a new land.

> "If you listen to these commands of the Lord your
>   God that I am giving you today, and if you
>   carefully obey them, the Lord will make you the
>   head and not the tail, and you will always be on
>   top and never at the bottom."

> — DEUTERONOMY 28:13

Deuteronomy 28:1-14 was written to tithers, and those who obey God's instructions.

> "The Lord your God will bless you as he has
>   promised. You will lend money to many nations
>   but will never need to borrow. You will rule
>   many nations, but they will not rule over you."

> — DEUTERONOMY 15:6

Psalm 37:11 says that the righteous will possess the land. When our ministry was trying to acquire property, we had our first property within a year, a second property in another year, and it has only continued. Two apartments, a dentist's office, two ministry offices, and more. All cash...no banks involved.

7. Tithing Brings Restoration

> "I am the LORD, and I do not change. That is why
>   you descendants of Jacob are not already
>   destroyed. Ever since the days of your ancestors,

you have scorned my decrees and failed to obey them. Now return to me, and I will return to you," says the LORD of Heaven's Armies.

— MALACHI 3: 6-7

"Now return to me in the tithe and the offering and see if I won't." They were in rebellion and under a curse. They returned to God in the tithe and the offering, and it caused the curse to dissipate and the blessing to take over.

Tithing brings restoration.

8. Tithers Protect Their Nation

They could not collapse the United States economy in 2020 because there are too many tithers. Tithers protect their nation.

I'm accustomed to preaching this. But it still stuns me how many Christians tell me that during the lockdown, financially speaking, they had the best year they ever had.

The global reset can't work in a nation where the people tithe and give offerings because they're not in that system. You can't shut them down. You can't take their money and force them into socialism.

9. Your Income Today Will Be Your Tithe Tomorrow

In 2012 our total gross income for our ministry was $100,000. In 2016, a man put a million dollars in the offering. Now I tithe $100,000 from one week's income.

If you continue tithing, your income today will be your tithe tomorrow. What takes you all year to bring in, will be 10% off what you get in one check in the future.

Does the Bible not say, *"See if I won't return a hundredfold of what you give?"*

> When the Lord brought back his exiles to Jerusalem,
>   it was like a dream!
> We were filled with laughter, and we sang for joy.
> And the other nations said, "What amazing things
>   the Lord has done for them."
> Yes, the Lord has done amazing things for us!
> What joy!
> Restore our fortunes, Lord, as streams renew the
>   desert.
> Those who plant in tears will harvest with shouts
>   of joy.
> They weep as they go to plant their seed, but they
>   sing as they return with the harvest.

— PSALM 126:1-6

"Those that sow in tears will reap with shouts of joy."

They're quiet because the Lord is speaking to them about precious seeds. You don't shout when the Lord is telling you to sow precious seed. But those that sow in tears will reap with shouts of joy. They cry as they plant their seed, but they return singing with their harvest.

If you don't feel what leaves your hand, you won't feel what comes back into your life. But if you *feel* what leaves your hand, you will *feel* what comes back into your life.

LESSON 7

ABRAHAM COULD ONLY RECEIVE AS FAR AS HE COULD SEE

F ew modern-day believers understand the subject of dominion. For example, when presidential leadership recently changed hands in the United States, you'd have thought Jesus died.

Abraham is called our *Father* in the faith. Abraham did not busy himself with what the heathen nation was doing. Abraham focused on setting up his family and his wealth and walking out his destiny. As a believer, that's the mentality you must have.

It doesn't matter who's in charge of the nation because God is for you, and the plans of evil against you won't prosper. Evil plans don't just automatically disappear, but the Lord will always route you around them.

> So Abram left Egypt and traveled north into the
> Negev, along with his wife and Lot and all that
> they owned. (Abram was very rich in livestock,
> silver, and gold.) From the Negev, they continued
> traveling by stages toward Bethel, and they

pitched their tents between Bethel and Ai, where
they had camped before. This was the same place
where Abram had built the altar, and there he
worshiped the Lord again.

Lot, who was traveling with Abram, had also
become very wealthy with flocks of sheep and
goats, herds of cattle, and many tents. But the
land could not support both Abram and Lot with
all their flocks and herds living so close together.
So disputes broke out between the herdsmen of
Abram and Lot. (At that time Canaanites and
Perizzites were also living in the land.)

Finally Abram said to Lot, "Let's not allow this
conflict to come between us or our herdsmen.
After all, we are close relatives! The whole
countryside is open to you. Take your choice of
any section of the land you want, and we will
separate."

— GENESIS 13 1:9

The blessing of God does not make sense to your natural mind.
Someone can stuff your well with dirt, but you dig another well, and
you're more blessed than you were before.

This is the mentality of Abraham: "You pick any place you want; it
won't affect me. And then I'll pick whatever you don't pick, and I'll
keep shining."

You need to know that God has blessed you as a Christian, and man
cannot curse what God has blessed.

"...If you want the land to the left, then I'll take the
land on the right. If you prefer the land on the
right, then I'll go to the left."

— GENESIS 13 1:9

Whatever someone else does can't stop you. It's the equivalent of
taking a beach ball and pushing it under the water. Eventually,
you're going to have to let go, and the beach ball will pop up higher
than it was before. That's how you are as a child of God.

Lot took a long look at the fertile plains of the Jordan
Valley in the direction of Zoar. The whole area
was well watered everywhere, like the garden of
the Lord or the beautiful land of Egypt. (This was
before the Lord destroyed Sodom and
Gomorrah.) Lot chose for himself the whole
Jordan Valley to the east of them. He went there
with his flocks and servants and parted company
with his uncle Abram. So Abram settled in the
land of Canaan, and Lot moved his tents to a
place near Sodom and settled among the cities of
the plain.

— GENESIS 13:10-12

Note the difference between Abraham and Lot. Lot is attracted to
Sodom and *settled among the cities of the plain.* When we check
back on Lot, he has gone so far as to live *in* Sodom.

There's an old-preacher-saying: "Where you're looking today will be where you're living tomorrow." Pay attention to what you're attracted to because you need to be careful. Sin starts out small.

Look at Achan in Joshua 6:18-19

"Achan, why did you sin before the Lord?"

"I saw a bar of gold and some clothing. I wanted them. I took them. I hid them."

Sin goes in four stages: I saw, I coveted, I took, I hid.

People start dealing with problems in the taking part, but it all takes root in the "I saw" and "I coveted" parts. David saw Bathsheba. He wanted her, slept with her, and had her husband killed to cover it up. If you wait to address the problem until you reach the "took stage", you'll always stay in trouble and never get ahead.

Eyes are an entrance point to the heart, and ears are an entrance point to the heart. Guard carefully what you allow yourself to gaze upon and what you allow yourself to listen to because where you're looking today is where you'll be living tomorrow.

> So Abram settled in the land of Canaan, and Lot
> moved his tents to a place near Sodom and
> settled among the cities of the plain. But the
> people of this area were extremely wicked and
> constantly sinned against the Lord.
> After Lot had gone, the Lord said to Abram, "Look
> as far as you can see in every direction—north
> and south, east and west. I am giving all this
> land, as far as you can see..."
> "...to you and your descendants as a permanent
> possession. And I will give you so many

descendants that, like the dust of the earth, they
cannot be counted! Go and walk through the
land in every direction, for I am giving it to
you."

So Abram moved his camp to Hebron and settled
near the oak grove belonging to Mamre. There he
built another altar to the Lord.

— GENESIS 13:12-18

"I'm giving you as far as you can see." This is a compelling point.

Based on what Lot was choosing to focus on, he went to live in Sodom. But Abraham built an altar to the Lord—two very different stories.

I want you to get this concept rooted into your heart: *What I can't see, I'll never have.* When you don't see healing in the Bible, sickness becomes a struggle. When you don't see prosperity in the Bible, money is a struggle. Anything you don't see, you'll never have.

When I saw the scripture in Psalm 37, *the righteous will possess the land,* I saw it in my spirit. I saw that, as a believer, I have a scriptural right to be a landowner. Now we own a lot of land and property. Before that, I had never owned any land, and I probably never would have if I didn't build my faith on the Word of God.

You can only receive as far as you can see.

WHAT YOU SEE DETERMINES WHAT YOU POSSESS

Some people only see struggle. The news puts struggle on, they watch struggle, and they receive what they see. They begin to think everybody is struggling. They start to talk about struggling. Then they only see obstacles, so they receive obstacles.

I met a missionary from the UK, and after he heard me preach, he wrote-off everything I said because I'm in America. He said, "In England, there are no churches with over 80 people."

I asked him, "Have you ever heard of Matthew Ashimolowo?"

"No." he said.

"I figured you hadn't. Matthew Ashimolowo has the largest church in Western Europe. Thousands of people attend every Sunday."

"Oh, I never knew that."

"Of course, you didn't because you have never seen a successful ministry in the UK. So you'll never have a successful ministry in the UK."

How come I knew about the top church in England and he didn't as a missionary to the Brits? Because I've made it a point to seek out successful people in my generation and put what they're doing before my eyes. Because I've seen Pastor Paul Enenche's new 100,000-seat church, now I can see what's possible.

Additionally, now I don't think something is a big deal when it's really not that big of a deal. If I were to build a 500-seat building and it was filled, I wouldn't think I had a remarkable church. I'd feel like I'm getting close to level one of the ladder because there's a man in Nigeria with a 100,000-seat church.

WHAT YOU SEE DETERMINES WHAT YOU BECOME

> This book of the law shall not depart out of thy
>   mouth; but thou shalt meditate therein day and
>   night, that thou mayest observe to do according
>   to all that is written therein: for then thou shalt
>   make thy way prosperous, and then thou shalt
>   have good success.
>
> — JOSHUA 1:8 (KJV)

I want you to get this in your heart: *What I observe is what I will do.*

When Peter raised Dorcas from the dead in Acts 9, he basically did exactly what Jesus did when he raised Jairus' daughter from the dead. Peter saw how Jesus raised the girl from the dead and then repeated the steps.

The ministers that see deaf ears open don't ask God to do it. They put their fingers in the ears and command the deafness to come out and the ears to open. A minister that's never seen somebody open the ears of the deaf doesn't even know how to pray for the deaf. You know how to do something because of what you observe.

You only receive what you see, which is why what you set before your eyes is so important. This is not just to keep negative things out of your meditation; this also enables you to observe the top performer in fields you want to dominate.

Who's the top performer in your field or mission? For example, if you're an evangelist, who's the top evangelist? In my opinion, Dag Heward-Mills, is the top evangelist. Prior to him, it's Reinhard

Bonnke and Billy Graham. You're a fool if you're an evangelist and you don't watch those people.

Why do you know who the best basketball player is, but you don't play basketball? Yet you don't know who the best evangelist is, and you're an evangelist?

It's your job to seek them out and look. You don't have to fly there, though I have. All you have to do is watch it on YouTube. Watch the best of it.

As far as you can see is what I'll give you. If you can't see it, you can't have it.

When we do our outdoor crusades, people say, "We want to do an outdoor crusade, and we want you to be the preacher." I won't do it unless I'm the one running it. Their idea of an outdoor crusade is not my idea of an outdoor crusade. I'm looking to have what Bonnke had in Nigeria but in the United States. I haven't hit anywhere close to that yet, but that's where I'm headed because that's what I've seen and put before my eyes.

DON'T FOCUS ON THE OBSTACLES

Where is your focus? Do you focus on obstacles? If so, you'll only see obstacles.

Many only see poverty. I had a minister I was preaching for say, "There's no money in this town." As he was saying it, we were driving by a Maserati dealership.

I said, "Are only people from out of town allowed to buy cars there?"

You know what he said? "I never noticed that dealership before."

When your eyes gravitate towards defeat, you miss everything.

I can tell by the way some ministers receive an offering. They think everybody is poor. There are people in your congregation that will plop down $5,000 at a casino and be done with it in 20 minutes. Not everyone is struggling. Your eyes should be able to see provision and blessing around you.

Learn to look for reward. God didn't say He'd curse us for obeying Him. He said He would reward us for obedience. You should look for reward. Look for positive things.

SEE RICHES

You can only receive what you see. If your eyes have only seen low-level things, you'll shoot for low-level things. Get your mind thinking in a higher direction.

That song that Israel Houghton recorded: "No Limits" has lyrics that read, "I see increase all around me." That song is anointed; you should learn to look around like that in your life.

When someone drives through a city, and they see commercial properties for sale everywhere, they see an economy in decline. But I see property available for pennies on the dollar and an opportunity to increase.

Look at what the best is. Then like a bee, going to different flowers, take the pollen from those things you've seen, and build your own honeycomb. Now, me looking at a $300,000 watch doesn't mean I'm going to start focusing my life around how to get it. But I want to know what heathen people have under a curse because I should have faith to go at that level under a blessing.

If you want to build a church that can seat 300, and you start looking at a church that seats 100,000, all of a sudden, you're like, "Oh man, that's nothing. I should be able to do that." Whereas if you've never seen that, and you've only seen churches that have 600, you're like, "I need the Lord's help." But if you start looking at high things, it's like, "The thing I'm believing for is next to nothing." When you look higher, things that used to be high don't seem so high anymore.

Oftentimes what you think is a big deal to believe God for is actually low. If the Lord could speak to us today, He would tell us what He told Abraham, "Lift up your eyes. Start looking for the best, not what's cheapest."

The desire for more is innate and will never go away because we're created in the image of God. God has an increasing nature, and He put the desire in us to increase. That's a God nature that the Devil can pervert into greed, but it doesn't have to be perverted.

Most Christians don't even know where the top is or how to look for more. Lift up your eyes.

The financial anointing is not only real, it's extremely important. A case in point is a minister who preaches 10 times better than I do, but if I have 100 times more money, I can have more people at my meeting with more people saved.

There's many preachers with a powerful miracle ministry, powerful word delivery, powerful altar calls, and low funds. They might be able to put an event together with 250 people and have 80 people come to the altar. Almost a third of the crowd comes forward to receive Jesus Christ. Then there's the other minister, with lesser preaching skills, lesser anointing, BUT has the financial anointing to put a crusade together with 40,000 people. He only gets a 1% response but has 400 at the altar.

It's difficult to grasp the full scope of Abrahamic wealth. Abraham owned vast pieces of land and had his own water supply. God could only give Abraham what he saw. What you see determines where you go and what you go for.

When God told Solomon, "I will make you rich," Solomon was already rich.

I want you to get this concept down: *I see increase all around me. I see a higher level.*

I traveled to see Bishop David Oyedepo's church in Nigeria because I wanted to see it. My life would lack something if I had never seen that in person. There are things you need to see in person. It does something for your faith. You can feel your insides expand. You can feel your mind get bigger and focus on the possibilities.

What have you seen? You shouldn't just take trips for vacations. You should schedule trips to see the big things in your field.

If you're having a building constructed, search for and visit the best building on planet Earth, similar to the the one you're building.

See it. It will do something for you. You will go higher.

LESSON 8

ABRAHAM'S PRINCIPLES FOR DOMINATION

A braham was not concerned about what his enemy was doing. Abraham had a plan from God and prospered, even in harsh climates. He was never concerned with what the heathen rulers were doing. He dominated in that nation.

ABRAHAM LAID UP AN INHERITANCE

> Good people leave an inheritance to their
>   grandchildren,
> but the sinner's wealth passes to the godly.
>
> — PROVERBS 13:22

Abraham had a mindset to lay up an inheritance for future generations and leave something on the earth so that his children didn't have to fight the same battles he fought.

From an Abrahamic perspective, it is ridiculous for your child to start at eighteen-years-old where you were at eighteen. Abraham left behind land, livestock, wells, silver, and gold. Not only did he leave a physical inheritance, but he left a spiritual inheritance. He showed them the way forward.

God has always planned and willed for His people to be free from poverty, weakness, and sickness and have an abundance of good things to enjoy. All the patriarchs of the Bible were healthy, wealthy, and wise. Look at Adam; he was the richest man that ever lived or ever will live. He owned the entire earth and everything in it. He was created to rule the sun, the moon, and the stars. When men inherit the earth again, many will own what Adam had before the fall.

Abraham was also very rich, owning enumerable flocks, herds, much silver and gold, and he had hundreds of servants. Psalm 16:9 says he had 318 soldiers—it takes a very wealthy man to support 318 trained soldiers and their wives and children.

Isaac inherited all that Abraham had, except portions given to the other sons sent into the east away from Isaac. He continued to add to his wealth and was considered more prosperous and more significant in power than the king of Philistia. We read that he was a successful farmer and had flocks, herds, and a great store of servants.

Jacob inherited the wealth and servants of both Abraham and Isaac, other than the portion given to Esau. He became very rich in his own right in Haran. He even gave Esau a token of friendship; 550 head of livestock when he met him, saying that it was nothing and he had plenty more.

Abraham is called the father of us all. Therefore, if God allowed him to be rich, we should not see our own prosperity as displeasing to God. The abundance of life for body, soul, and spirit is promised to every man in Christ today. It is God's will that all His children prosper and be in good health, even as their souls prosper (3 John 1:2).

ABRAHAM RAISED HIS FAMILY IN FEAR AND ADMONITION OF GOD

> And the Lord said, Shall I hide from Abraham that
> thing which I do; Seeing that Abraham shall
> surely become a great and mighty nation, and all
> the nations of the earth shall be blessed in him?
> For I know him, that he will command his
> children and his household after him, and they
> shall keep the way of the Lord, to do justice and
> judgment; that the Lord may bring upon
> Abraham that which he hath spoken of him.
>
> — GENESIS 18:17-19 (KJV)

Abraham raised his family in fear and admonition of God. This is a secret to Abraham's greatness that you can't dance around. It attracted God's favor. *I know him. He will command his family to keep the ways of the Lord.* Can God say that about you?

My wife loves God with her own heart. My daughter loves God with her own heart. They're not forced to love God. But if it came down to it, they would be forced to worship God while they're in my house.

I was never given the opportunity to not go to church. Dad never said to me, "Hey, it's Sunday. If you want to come to church, we're all going." The only way I was allowed to miss church was if I was throwing up. And then once I threw up, my dad would say, "There, you threw up. Now you're okay to go to church."

That's something the older generation did that you don't see my generation doing. Instead, Dad or Mom will just head out to church by themselves.

"I know Abraham will command his family to keep My ways. Therefore, I'm going to entrust Abraham with generational wealth because he's going to train and command his family to keep My ways and he's going to train his generations to do what he does."

ABRAHAM HAD A PERSONAL, UNSHAKABLE COMMITMENT TO GOD

Abraham had an unshakeable commitment to God. In Genesis 13, Lot went to Sodom. Lot pitched his tent towards Sodom. But Abraham built an altar. Abraham paid Melchizedek first before he paid his men. Abraham left his father's home the same day the Lord spoke to him.

Oh, the joys of those who do not follow the advice of
the wicked, or stand around with sinners, or join
in with mockers. But they delight in the law of
the Lord, meditating on it day and night. They
are like trees planted along the riverbank, bearing
fruit each season. Their leaves never wither, and
they prosper in all they do.

— PSALM 1:1-3

I want you to get this concept down: Godliness carries its own reward.

The righteous are like a tree planted along the riverbank; in every season, they bear fruit (Psalm 1:3). Godliness carries a threefold reward:

In every season, they bear fruit—no dry seasons.

In every season, they bear fruit, and their leaves never wither—no regression.

Whatsoever he does, it shall prosper—everything you touch is blessed.

ABRAHAM OBEYED GOD WITH SPEED

When he heard the Lord give him an instruction, he did it immediately.

In your relationship with God, you lose more by moving slowly than you do by moving quickly. Every time God spoke to Abraham, you'll read the Bible say: "And immediately," or "That same day."

God spoke to Abraham and said, *"Get thee out of thy father's house and away from your family and go to the land that I will show you."* He didn't even tell him where he was going. He was married and had roots put down in his life. Yet, that same day, Abraham departed.

The only time you don't see him move immediately is when God told him to sacrifice Isaac. The Bible says, *"Early the next morning."* All the other times, Abraham never waited more than 24 hours to obey God and usually did it within the day.

God moves quickly. The Holy Spirit didn't come as a slow southern breeze. He came in like a mighty rushing wind. When the Lord speaks to you, there's a zeal and a joy that accompanies His instruction that gives you the energy to get it done quickly. When He speaks to you, whatever He tells you to do, do it, and do it now. I have seen many people miss God's best for their lives because they were too slow.

Reinhard Bonnke said, "God works with the workers, goes with the goers but does not sit with the sitters."

The first word of the Great Commission is GO. Everything changed for the lepers in 2 Kings when they said, *"Why sit here till we die? Let's go."*

On December 31, God spoke to me to make a big move in our ministry. Most of the delay was waiting on other people, the kind involved when you make a big move. But if it was up to me, it would have been done in an hour.

When I had the privilege to meet Dag Heward-Mills, I said, "If you were in my position and at my age, what would you say?" He said, "I always move quickly."

When the Lord opens a door, go through it. The opportunity of a lifetime must be seized in the lifetime of the opportunity. If you dilly-dally, and it passes you by, it doesn't come back.

When God said, *"Get thee out of thy father's home and away from your kindred and go to the land that I'll show you,"* Abraham could have said, "Okay, let me just talk to Sarah because I know she has a birthday party planned this coming week. She has brunch with some of the women in town, and I know she was really looking forward to it."

Instead, Abraham was like, "Sarah, we're going. Let's go." That's how he ran his home. He wasn't married to some rebellious heathen woman like a lot of Christians are. God doesn't speak to multiple leaders, God speaks to the head, and the husband is the head of the home.

I heard a minister say this: "I felt the Lord open a door for us to pastor a church. I knew it was God, but we didn't end up going because my wife said she didn't want to live more than 50 miles away from her mother, because her mother needs somebody to take care of her." Small people stay small for the same reasons.

Remember, delayed obedience is disobedience.

ABRAHAM LOVED SOULS

We all have the same favor available to us. But not everyone walks in the same level of favor. There are actions men take that engender God's favor.

> The other men turned and headed toward Sodom, but the Lord remained with Abraham. Abraham approached him and said, "Will you sweep away both the righteous and the wicked? Suppose you find fifty righteous people living there in the city —will you still sweep it away and not spare it for their sakes? Surely you wouldn't do such a thing, destroying the righteous along with the wicked. Why, you would be treating the righteous and the wicked exactly the same! Surely you wouldn't do that! Should not the Judge of all the earth do what is right?"
> And the Lord replied, "If I find fifty righteous people

in Sodom, I will spare the entire city for their sake."

Then Abraham spoke again. "Since I have begun, let me speak further to my Lord, even though I am but dust and ashes. Suppose there are only forty-five righteous people rather than fifty? Will you destroy the whole city for lack of five?"

And the Lord said, "I will not destroy it if I find forty-five righteous people there."

Then Abraham pressed his request further. "Suppose there are only forty?"

And the Lord replied, "I will not destroy it for the sake of the forty."

"Please don't be angry, my Lord," Abraham pleaded. "Let me speak—suppose only thirty righteous people are found?"

And the Lord replied, "I will not destroy it if I find thirty."

Then Abraham said, "Since I have dared to speak to the Lord, let me continue—suppose there are only twenty?"

And the Lord replied, "Then I will not destroy it for the sake of the twenty."

Finally, Abraham said, "Lord, please don't be angry with me if I speak one more time. Suppose only ten are found there?"

And the Lord replied, "Then I will not destroy it for the sake of the ten."

> When the Lord had finished his conversation with
> Abraham, he went on his way, and Abraham
> returned to his tent.
>
> — GENESIS 18:22-33

Abraham loved souls. He didn't want them to perish; he wanted them to be saved. He wasn't looking forward to Sodom and Gomorrah getting burned to the ground. He tried to stop it, even though they were terrible people.

I want you to get this concept down: There's prosperity in soul winning.

The highest thing you can ever do is rise up and give yourself to win the lost and win people to Jesus Christ. The laborers are paid good wages. The crops they harvest are souls being brought to eternal life (John 4:36). Righteousness carries its own material reward, and so does soul winning.

ABRAHAM SPENT HIS TIME LAUGHING WITH THE JOY OF THE PROMISES, NOT CRYING ABOUT THE OPPOSITION'S THREATS

> Abraham was 100 years old when Isaac was born.
> And Sarah declared, "God has brought me laughter.
> All who hear about this will laugh with me."
>
> — GENESIS 21:5-6

In Abraham's house, they were laughing at 100 years old.

127

Jesus, knowing the joy that was set before Him, endured the shame, reproach, and indignity of the cross.

To walk in Abrahamic dominance, you must have the joy of the Holy Ghost as your engine. Sorrow kills, but joy makes a life. Never allow anything to steal your joy. The joy of the Lord is your strength (Nehemiah 8:10). You don't focus on threats against you. You focus on God being for you.

If God is for you, who can be against you?

Sorrow is the atmosphere that Satan lives in; joy is the atmosphere of the Holy Ghost.

> A merry heart doeth good like a medicine: but a
> broken spirit drieth the bones.
>
> — PROVERBS 17:22(KJV)

> For the kingdom of God is not meat and drink; but
> righteousness, and peace, and joy in the Holy
> Ghost.
>
> — ROMANS 14:17 (KJV)

ABRAHAM BROKE FROM HIS FAMILY, WHO WOULD NOT COME ALONG

Abraham valued covenant over sentiment. Some people are overly sentimental. If you stay like that, you'll struggle to serve God, and you won't operate in Abrahamic dominance.

In Genesis 12:1-3, the whole thing started with, *"Get thee out of thy father's home, away from thy kin and your country."* You must break out of the old to step into the new. The old wineskin can't hold new wine. You can't be overly sentimental about the old stuff.

When you try to step into healing, you'll have family trying to talk you out of it. When you try to step into prosperity, you'll have family angry that you're prospering. At that point, you're going to have to make up your mind whether you're willing and obedient or just obedient. If you are willing and obedient, you'll eat the good of the land.

Some people are obedient, but they're not willing to endure the persecution that comes with rising to the top. When your father buys you a coat of many colors, not all your brothers will be happy about it.

> ...Jesus replied, "and I assure you that everyone who
> has given up house or brothers or sisters or
> mother or father or children or property, for my
> sake and for the Good News, will receive now in
> return a hundred times as many houses, brothers,
> sisters, mothers, children, and property—along
> with persecution. And in the world to come that
> person will have eternal life."
>
> — MARK 10:29-30

That verse is not there by accident.

The harder you press into God, the more people you lose. People get offended at your love for God, even your family—even if they are Christians.

Christian families can fight the worst. To an unsaved family, it's just this weird little thing you're into; they don't know about doctrine, and they don't believe in any of it. But if your family has just enough of the Bible to make them dangerous and 40% commitment to God, when you start taking it seriously, they are the first to have issues with your decisions.

Abraham broke from his family, who would not come along. Jewish tradition says that Abraham's father, Terah, not only worshiped idols, but he was also an idol manufacturer.

There are people you must break away from to enter into Abrahamic dominance. You can't bring everybody along for the ride because not everybody is interested.

ABRAHAM GOT TO WORK

Diligent work draws the favor of God and spirituality is no substitute for diligent work.

God told Abraham, *"I will make you rich and I'm going to make you so blessed that all the nations of the earth will be blessed through you."* What did Abraham do after that? He understood that the work of his hands was the primary channel through which God's blessing would flow. So, he got to work. He ranched cattle, he dug wells, he had servants, built a legacy, and prepared an inheritance.

Bishop Oyedepo said, "You have two choices in life: hard work or a hard life."

If you want to be like your father Abraham, you will do the works that Abraham did. The revelation of grace is not a revelation that gets you to be a lazy bum.

But those who won't care for their relatives,
  especially those in their own household, have
  denied the true faith. Such people are worse than
  unbelievers.

— 1 TIMOTHY 5:8

The apostle Paul taught the New Testament church: *"A man who doesn't provide for his family has left the faith and is worse than an infidel."*

God hates laziness and despises lazy men. Knowledge of God's word is not a substitute for diligent work. Abraham got to work and he didn't use spirituality as a substitute for digging wells or ranching cattle and sheep.

ABRAHAM REFUSED TO BORROW

For the Lord thy God blesseth thee, as he promised
  thee: and thou shalt lend unto many nations, but
  thou shalt not borrow.

— DEUTERONOMY 15:6 (KJV)

Thou shalt not borrow.

You will never dominate like Abraham dominated until you take the steps Abraham took. Not many teach this, but it is a major key to prosperity, to the Abrahamic blessing, and to receiving what the Bible says belongs to you in Proverbs 10:22, *"The blessing of the Lord makes a man rich and he addeth no sorrow."*

If you're going to do what Abraham did, you're going to have to buck the harshest pressure in the West (America, Canada, and Europe). Often you are forced to borrow. They want to make you an economic slave to the lending system and to the interest and debt system. You have to make up your mind that you're going to operate outside of that system, just like Abraham.

LESSON 9

ABRAHAM WASN'T A SLAVE TO DEBT

"Do not take interest or any profit from them, but
fear your God, so that they may continue to live
among you. You must not lend them money at
interest or sell them food at a profit."

— LEVITICUS 25:36-37 (NIV)

The Bible says godliness with contentment is great gain, but Godliness with discontentment brings great pain (1 Timothy 6:6). Your discontentment is a bad thing. If you get discontent in your marriage, it's the seed for an affair. If you get discontent with what the Lord has given you and covet something that isn't yours, it's the seed that gets you into the world's debt system. Borrowing is a false option when presented to you as a Christian. It's so attractive because it's an easy way to get what you want right now, but it's a trap.

Many Christian leaders are in debt up to their eyeballs. At the same time, they have buildings and property, visually appearing to be doing something. Then you have other people that brag about how they're debt-free, but they don't own anything. They've had the same small storefront church for 20 years with 30 people. They're debt-free, but they've built very little. Neither of these people believe God has a way to make them the lender and not the borrower; neither believe God has a way to bring them to the place where He wants them to be. God said, "I will bless you," and, *"I will make you the lender only, but thou shalt not borrow."*

> Unless the Lord builds a house, the work of the
>   builders is wasted.
> Unless the Lord protects a city, guarding it with
>   sentries will do no good.

— PSALM 127:1

God is a builder. If you do things correctly, you'll never build for God. Instead, you'll watch God build for you and turn things around. The Bible says that if God is not building it, your labor is in vain, which means there's a way to have God build. When God builds it, the stress is removed. Bishop David Oyedepo has a powerful statement on this subject; "If God can't give it to me, may I never have it. If God can't do it, let it remain undone. If God can't take me there, I don't want to go."

Once you get God's Word in your spirit, the entrance of His words brings light, and light drives out darkness. I caught the light of God's Word from Bishop David Oyedepo that I never have to borrow—It's anti-covenant. God will do the same thing for you.

BORROWING IS ANTI-COVENANT

Borrowing is against the covenant with God because God told His people that they would lend only and not borrow. But what do so many do? They get a loan anyways. If the Lord laid on your heart to get a property and He told you that you'll lend only and not borrow, why is your first thought to go borrow? Your Christianity will change if you start to believe that there's an actual God who's all-powerful and is willing and able to do this for you. When you believe that, it will change your life.

Borrowing is anti-covenant—Deuteronomy 15:6 and Deuteronomy 28:1-14 make it clear.

I'll make you the head and never the tail, above and always beneath, blessed in the city, blessed in the field, blessed when you come in, blessed when you go out again. I'll make you the lender only and never borrow.

BORROWING IS NOT A SIN, BUT THE BORROWER IS SERVANT TO THE LENDER

Borrowing works against your covenant, but the Bible never says that borrowing is a sin. However, it is a weight, and the Bible tells you to lay aside and strip off every weight that so easily ensnares you.

> ...the rich rule the poor, so the borrower is servant to the lender.

> — PROVERBS 22:7

The majority of people I meet in the ministry are not having fun. They're very stressed-out individuals because the Lord isn't doing it; the banks are doing it. The bank is very friendly when getting you to take a loan, but the relationship changes after that. They will send people to your work and dress you down in front of people for being late with their payment, and they'll treat you as their servant. The borrower is the slave of the person who lends to him, and as Christians, the only person we are to be a slave of is Christ. When did Abraham take a loan to do anything? He didn't. You cannot find a single place in the Bible where Abraham borrowed to do anything he was doing. Find for me where Isaac borrowed. Find for me where Jacob borrowed. You won't find it. It's not in our covenant.

An excellent pastor with a large church got sick with cancer, and he didn't want to take chemotherapy. He wanted to do a natural health regimen to knock the cancer out, but his bank wouldn't let him because he borrowed to buy his church property. When you do that in the ministry, the bank will usually do a "key man" insurance policy. This is where the bank concludes, "Okay, this thing hinges on him. If he dies, this thing is over. So, we're going to take out insurance on his life to guarantee the loan." That's what they did in his case. Because of the key man insurance policy, the bank legally had the right to force him to get chemotherapy, even though he was opposed to it. To get the loan to buy his church, he had to agree to that insurance policy, which gave the bank oversight over his personal life, including making health decisions.

When I heard this, it forever destroyed any desire I had to ever take a loan for any reason. I'll wear the same shirt for the rest of my life before borrowing money to get a second shirt. It's not up to me to build something big for the Lord; it's up to me to obey Him. He knows when I require more space or resources as things grow. I get my plans from Him, and I get my finances from Him. My sowing provokes the money.

UNDERSTAND THE ISHMAEL PRINCIPLE

Was it a sin for Abraham to have Ishmael? No. Rather, Ishmael represents what happens when God gives you a promise, and you make it happen in the flesh rather than in the spirit. For example, if the Lord spoke to me to build a 5,000-seat auditorium, that's what He is leading me towards. But if I get a loan and go on TV to do fundraisers to try to make it happen, I'm going towards what God told me would come, but I'm using the flesh to get there. This causes trouble, just as Ishmael did. If Abraham had waited, God would have given him a son by the Spirit, by his miracle-working power. Ishmael represents people's natural tendency to make their God-given dream happen in the flesh. When you do that, there's a price to pay. However, if you wait on the Lord, He pays the price.

Did God stop Abraham from having Ishmael? No. God will allow you the opportunity to birth an Ishmael before you receive Isaac. He'll see whether you'll take the bait or not, and that's where people often miss the mark. God will let you if you want to operate in an anti-covenant mindset. You won't go to hell, and He won't be mad at you, but you don't have to do it, and it's not in His plan for you.

People borrow because they have a need or think they lack something. They need a car. They need furniture. They need a washing machine. They need a home. They need office space. God promises that if you make the Lord your shepherd, you will never lack anything. From a covenant perspective, a Christian does not need to borrow. Abraham never borrowed. Abraham didn't ask the

Philistines or Canaanites if he could have an ox. Isaac never borrowed. Jacob never borrowed. They never borrowed because it's in our covenant to only lend and never borrow.

THE STOREHOUSE PRINCIPLE

This is not an excuse to never do or have anything, and this does not take away from your command to multiply and increase. The goal of Christianity is not to simply be debt-free. Being debt-free gives you more opportunities to help people, but it is not an accomplishment in itself. God didn't just say, "I'll make you lend to many, but thou shall not borrow," He said, "I'll fill your storehouse with green." This is the Storehouse Principle.

When my Uncle Ted first started in the ministry, he lived with his dad, a preacher, and my grandfather. My grandfather took my Uncle Ted's car to drive it and when he came home, he said, "Hey, Ted, how come every time I drive your car, the gas gauge is on E (empty)?" My uncle confidently replied, "Because I'm a faith preacher." For some reason, people for decades have equated faith with lack.

Abraham lived by faith, and was he broke because he lived by faith? Or was he loaded down with silver and gold? Stop using faith as a synonym for poverty! Faith is not a synonym for poverty. Faith is productive. Faith produces wealth. Faith produces healing. Faith produces the goodness of God in the land of the living.

In response to my Uncle Ted, my grandfather said, "It takes more faith to keep it on F (full) than it does E (empty)." God didn't say, "I'll meet your need only," He said, "I'll fill your storehouse with green." That means before any need arises, the provision will be there ahead of time. Wherever you are reading from, thank God that the provision will be there ahead of time before any need arises.

That's what it means to have a full storehouse. You don't pray for meals on the table when your storehouse is full, and neither do you make Facebook posts asking people to donate for something you planned. Money should not be requested from the standpoint of need. Paul appealed based on the principle of sowing and reaping in *2 Corinthians 8:9, "You know the generous grace of our Lord Jesus Christ. Though he was rich, yet for your sakes he became poor, so that by his poverty he could make you rich,"* and so did Elijah with the widow.

I hear stories like, "We owed $99,000. We had $98,000. Then in the last hour, we got the final $1,000, and we paid it off." But how much do you have now? Zero. That's no testimony. That's not Abraham. That's not Bible covenant—that's a disgrace. Drive the concept that faith means having less and barely getting by until God comes through in the midnight hour out of your spirit and out of your brain. What the church has celebrated as prosperity and provision is actually neither. It's far below where God's blessing and covenant entitle you to live.

You'll never be broke another day in your life. The blessing of God that made Abraham's cup overflow will cause your cup to overflow from today forward. The Devil can't do anything about it. From today onward, on the authority of God's Word, you lend only, but you'll never borrow. The Bible says so. God's Word works in every generation, in every nation, and for any person that will work it. If you got wrapped in an Ishmael-type financial relationship, God can break that and deal with it.

Today, you should ask the Lord what magnanimous seed He wants you to sow based on this revelation. When you hear something from the Word of God, and it jumps in your spirit, especially in the realm of finances, when you sow a seed towards that thing, you're taking action on the Word, and that always produces results. The widow didn't know that in 1 Kings 17, so Elijah focused her faith, showing her that when you give, the cruse of oil and the jar of meal shall not fail (1 Kings 17:14).

AFTERWORD

"Listen to me, all who hope for deliverance—all who
    seek the Lord! Consider the rock from which you
    were cut, the quarry from which you were mined.
    Yes, think about Abraham, your ancestor, and
    Sarah, who gave birth to your nation. Abraham
    was only one man when I called him. But when I
    blessed him, he became a great nation." The Lord
    will comfort Israel again and have pity on her
    ruins. Her desert will blossom like Eden, her
    barren wilderness like the garden of the Lord.
    Joy and gladness will be found there. Songs of
    thanksgiving will fill the air.

                                            — ISAIAH 51:1-3

Our spiritual root is in Abraham, and he dominated in a wicked
nation. Abraham wasn't part of a large body of believers like we are
today; instead, he was the only righteous man on the planet at that

time. Yet, he didn't focus on what the Philistines were doing but focused on obeying God. In doing so, Abraham became a great nation and dominated.

THE SEED OF ABRAHAM

"Abraham was only one man when I called him. But when I blessed him, he became a great nation."

— ISAIAH 51:2

The key to becoming a nation in one man is to *"consider the rock from which you were cut,"* and realize that you share spiritual DNA with Abraham. God says to consider yourself the seed of Abraham, which is the secret to staying in victory. While the Devil wants you to focus on your ethnicity, ethnic background means nothing, and spiritual lineage is everything. God wants you to connect to the spiritual DNA of Abraham.

In the same way, "Abraham believed God, and God counted him as righteous because of his faith." The real children of Abraham, then, are those who put their faith in God.

— GALATIANS 3:6-7

Just like Abraham, the potential to become a one-man or one-woman nation is inside of you. The blessing of God brings it alive and to fruition in your life.

BLESSING BY FAITH

> And now that you belong to Christ, you are the true
> children of Abraham. You are his heirs, and
> God's promise to Abraham belongs to you.
>
> — GALATIANS 3:29

Abraham's righteousness and blessing were attained by faith in God and faith in God's Word. Every overcomer lives by the faith of Abraham. When this becomes real to you, you'll distance yourself from strugglers and turn into a nation.

The true seeds of Abraham are those who put their faith in God. You activate the blessing through faith. Claim what's yours; activating God's blessing is about your faith in God.

Everything God promised to Abraham belongs to you. The blessing is extended to you and to me. You can access it regardless of your race, ethnicity, gender, or anything else. When you shift focus to your spiritual lineage and activate God's blessing through faith, it is impossible for racial, gender, or socioeconomic divisions to stop you from obtaining what God says is yours.

"MY GENERATION SHALL BE SAVED!"

— JONATHAN
SHUTTLESWORTH

ABOUT THE AUTHOR

Evangelist and Pastor, Jonathan Shuttlesworth, is the founder of Revival Today and Pastor of Revival Today Church, ministries dedicated to reaching lost and hurting people with The Gospel of Jesus Christ.

In fulfilling his calling, Jonathan Shuttlesworth has conducted meetings and open-air crusades throughout North America, India, the Caribbean, and Central and South Africa.

Revival Today Church was launched in 2022 as a soul-winning, Holy Spirit honoring church that is unapologetic about believing the Bible to bless families and nations.

Each day thousands of lives are impacted globally through Revival Today Broadcasting and Revival Today Church, located in Pittsburgh, Pennsylvania.

While methods may change, Revival Today's heartbeat remains for the lost, providing biblical teaching on faith, healing, prosperity, freedom from sin, and living a victorious life.

If you need help or would like to partner with Revival Today to see this generation and nation transformed through The Gospel, follow these links…

CONTACT REVIVAL TODAY

www.RevivalToday.com
www.RevivalTodayChurch.com

facebook.com/revivaltoday

twitter.com/jdshuttlesworth

instagram.com/jdshuttlesworth

youtube.com/RevivalToday07

CPSIA information can be obtained
at www.ICGtesting.com
Printed in the USA
BVHW082342110122
626006BV00001B/24